CANTOS FROM
DANTE'S INFERNO

DANTE ALIGHIERI

CANTOS FROM DANTE'S INFERNO

TRANSLATED BY ARMAND SCHWERNER

WITH THE TRANSLATOR'S PROCESS NOTES FOR
CANTOS VIII, IX, X, AND XXI

AND A PREFACE BY MICHAEL HELLER

TALISMAN HOUSE, PUBLISHERS
JERSEY CITY, NEW JERSEY

Copyright © 2000 by
the Literary Estate of Armand Schwerner
All rights reserved

Published in the United States of America by
Talisman House, Publishers
P.O. Box 3157
Jersey City, New Jersey 07303-3157

Manufactured in the United Sates of America
Printed on acid-free paper

Library of Congress Cataloging-in-Publication Data

Dante Alighieri, 1265-1321
   [Inferno, English]
   Cantos from Dante's inferno / [Dante Alighieri] ; translated by Armand Schwerner with the translator's process notes for Cantos VIII, IX, X, and XXI ; introduction by Michael Heller.
   p. cm.
   ISBN 1-883689-98-8 (cloth : alk. paper) — ISBN 1-883689-97-x (pbk. : alk. paper)
   I. Schwerner, Armand. II. Title.

PQ4315.2 .S39 1999
851'.1--dc21

                                      99-047639

CONTENTS

Preface by Michael Heller

Canto I

Canto II

Canto III

Canto IV

Canto V

Canto VI

Canto VII

Canto VIII

Canto IX

Canto X

Canto XV

Canto XXI

Translator's Process Notes to Cantos VIII, IX, X, and XXI

PREFACE

Michael Heller

    These translations by Armand Schwerner from Dante's *Inferno* attempt two interrelated tasks—to create a powerful figurative linguistic object, one that brings the powers of the original into the present, and at the same time to rescue the translation from the nostalgia that surrounds all translations of great works. Schwerner's aim in this *Inferno*, as he noted in his interview in *Talisman* #19, is to create "a direct confrontational sort of adventure" with Dante, one that seeks to avoid "the recycling of former English or American versions into the work." The reader notices immediately that the standard three-line approximation to *terza rime* of most verse translations of the *Commedia* has been abandoned, to be replaced by a prosodically tighter form, assigning narrative to the left side of the page, juxtaposing it with speech and oration on the right. This lineation, unlike other versions, and with perhaps a Bakhtinian dialogics in mind, focuses on the opposition between interior voicing of narration and rumination and the externality of speech, between psychic state and self-presentation. Dante's characters are still lodged in their assigned places, operating under the eye and plan of God—Dante's "Aquinas map," as Pound referred to it—but Schwerner's modality foregrounds a more contemporary linguistic and psychological dimension to their dramas. The ambiguity of their fates is now read, along with all the other factors, within the textual sphere, and with no loss of moral or spiritual depth.

    This impulse to re-envision is, well, Dantean, emulating the precursor's inventiveness, his break with prior form and his incorporation of a whole range of formerly unheard voices, demotics, and tonal ranges embedded in the Italian of his time. So too with Schwerner's American/English ideal, which is not so much colloquial as infused with the polyvalent, reflexive potentials of present-day speech and writing. Schwerner's working notes, published here for some of the cantos, are remarkable prose-poem-like forays and recuperations of living language. As they arc back and forth between Dante's Italian and Schwerner's English, they provide a fascinating exploration of word-choice, tone, and finally, artistic judgment. So, for example, the "Notes to Canto VIII," which shows the transiting between Dante's *"anima fella"* mistakenly shouted at Dante standing with Virgil by the boatman crossing the river and Schwerner's "galled soul" found in line 18 of the canto: Schwerner's entry takes us through Middle Eanglish, physiology, plant biology, and Virgil's aristocratic attitudinizing in order to take the "measure of the oarsman's demotic *now you've had it*. . . ." The kinetic energy released by these strenuous etymological excursions is both profound and entertaining. Profound and entertaining, and even quite comic, because one feels that Schwerner has, in this "direct confrontational adventure," gone for broke, scouring English's oddments and listening for the truth of cadence rather than meter—in other words, eschewing the weak or merely arbitrary submissiveness of past efforts. In this, his translation honors nothing so much as the vitality and directness of the original, and in this act of faithfulness to Dante, what comes over is a marvelous, nearly magical act of transmutation. As Serge Gavronsky exclaims in "On Dante's Way"—his brilliant note on Schwerner's translation in *Talisman* #19—"What a dictionary day, then, genetic criticism would have tracing Schwerner's becoming Dante in the fold of the American language!"

Clearly, Schwerner's untimely death before he could complete the entirety of his translation of the *Inferno* makes the cantos included here something of a work-in-progress. Undoubtedly, there would have been revisions and rebalancings as more cantos came into being. Still, the idiosyncratic power of what we have here, the great pleasure one gets out of Schwerner's play with both form and diction, reminds us of his peculiar brilliance as both poet and translator. To use one of his own favorite words, Schwerner has given us a translation full of "availabilities," entry points, and registers of our hopes and understandings, leading us both forward and back to the figure of Dante. What he aspires for in composing his poetry can be said of this translation, "There's no old or new in it as long as I'm in language's changing weathers." Such timeliness translates here as timeless—Dante's of course, but also Schwerner's.

CANTOS FROM
DANTE'S INFERNO

CANTO I

In the middle of the journey
of our life
I came to myself
in a dark forest
the straightforward way
misplaced.

Ah it's so hard to tell
about that wild
sour and rank wood—
at the thought of it
I'm afraid again, recall
so bitter, almost
beyond dying.
              But
to take up the good
I found in that place
I'll tell of the other things
I marked in that place.

So sleep-filled when I forsook the true way
I can't really say how I came to that place;
at the end of the valley where my heart
had been gashed by fear I got to the foot
of a hill and looking up saw its shoulders
cloaked by the light-shafts of the planet
which on every road leads men straight.
Then a little quiet came to the fear within the lake
of my heart, fear which had gone
on in the night I'd spent so heavy-laden.

And like a panting swimmer who
having attained shore from the deeps turns
toward the hazardous waters and gazes,
so my mind still in flight turned
back to look one more time at the pass
which had never allowed any to leave alive.

My spent body slightly rested I picked my way
again over the deserted slope, haltingly—
firm foot always the lower. And now! right after
the start of the climb: a swift lithe leopard
with a brindled hide so persistent in fronting me,
blocking my way, that again and again
I veered to leave.
                It was the start of the morning,
the sun with its attendant stars going up, beautiful
bodies first set in motion by Divine Love—
o the time and the sweet season so fed my good
hope to get free of that gaily dappled beast, but
I was frightened by the sudden sight of a lion,
on the attack I thought, its head high and so hunger-mad
the very air seemed afraid of it; and by a she-wolf
who seemed in its rawboned body fraught
with all cravings, and which has already bred
much misery in many.
                The terror I felt at the sight of her
induced in me a heaviness so great that my hope
for the climb was lost. There was no peace
in that beast; because of her I felt
like a man pleased with his winnings
who in time becomes a loser and sadly grieves.
She came at me and drove me step by step
back toward the place where the sun is silent.
While I was retreating down to the valley
and the obscure wood, my eyes made out a being
whose voice seemed dim through long quiet;
when I saw him in that barren site I cried to him:

"Take pity on me, whoever you are, shade
or real man."

He answered me:

"Not man; I was man once and my parents
were Lombards, both born in Mantua. I was born
late in the reign of Julius Caesar and lived
in Rome under the good Augustus in the time
of the false, lying gods. I was a poet; I sang
of Aeneas the just son of Anchises who came
from Troy after the burning of magnificent
Ilium. But you, why are you coming back
to such misery? Why not climb up the bliss-giving
mountain, beginning and cause of all joy?"

Shame capping my forehead, I answered him:

"Could you then be that Virgil, that fount
from which the great river of language rises? O
exultation and light of other poets, I so pondered
your book—if only my long search in it
and my great love for it can suffice—you
are my master and you are my author, for me
the only begetter of the raised style I took
and which has brought me honor. See
the she-wolf from whom I turned away.
O my blood trembles in its vessels—
esteemed sage, save me from that beast!"

When he saw me in tears he answered:

"To get away from this feral place you need
to take another road: this beast which made you
wail bars every man's passage, and kills.
Her nature is so evil and malignant nothing
can ever sate her avid craving; her meal consumed

she's hungrier after than before. She couples
with many beasts and will couple with many more
till brought to the throes of death by the hound.
For him no appetite for booty or land, only
for wisdom, love and gallantry, and his country
shall be between Feltro and Feltro. For low-lying
Italy the virgin Camilla died of her wounds
and so did Euryalus and Turnus and Nisus:
for that Italy will the hound be salvation.
And he will hunt the beast through every town
until she's driven back to Hell, from where
originally envy let her loose. So thinking of
the course that's best for you I conclude
that you should follow me and I will be your guide
and lead you from here through an eternal place
where you'll hear forlorn screeches and see
afflicted timeworn spirits screaming in the second death.

Then you'll see those content in Purgatory's shriving
fire who hope to reach the company of the blessed,
sometime. Climbing up there, if you want to, you'll find
a soul more fit than I; at my good-bye I'll leave you
to her—I rebelled against the reigning emperor's law,
and he *will* not let me in where, seat and city, he's
enthroned and governs. O the joy of the being he chooses!"

And I to him:

"Poet, so that I can run
from this evil or worse
I beg you
by that God you never knew
to lead me where you said
and let me see Saint Peter's gate
and those sad beings."

Then he moved on; I followed behind.

CANTO II

The departing day and the brown surround
were releasing earth's beings
from their work, and I, alone,
was getting ready to bear
the agony of the way
and of compassion for the damned
which memory, errorless, will depict.
O inspiriting Muses, O my own genial gift, now help me
O memory, that marked what I saw,
be here, magnanimous.

I began:

>"Poet, my guide
>before you loose me into the harsh
>transit, gauge my skillful means.
>Am I ready? You told the story:
>Sylvius's father Aeneas though still alive
>went to the otherworld;
>still if the Adversary of all evil
>was kind to *him,* any disinterested man—
>the profound results in Aeneas's seed
>revealed—would recognize
>suitability,
>>because in the outermost,
>Empyrean, Heaven, he was chosen to father
>Rome's soul and Rome's empire, both in truth
>established as the sacred spot
>of great Peter's successor, where he sits.
>Through this storied trip your words honor,
>things he heard would engender his victory
>and after that the papal cloak.

> Then Paul the chosen Vessel went to Heaven
> to bear from there solace of that faith
> which initiates the saving way.
> But I, why should I arrive there,
> the otherworld? through whose intercession?
> I'm not Aeneas; I'm not Paul:
> neither I nor anyone considers me
> worthy. So if I yield myself to this arrival,
> I also shrink from it as maybe crazy.
> *You're* wise; your understanding outstrips
> my reasoning."

On that obscure hilltop it was as if I'd
turned into a being who unwills what he'd willed
who with new thoughts alters his intention.
I backed out from what I'd started—
thought aborting act too hurriedly entered on
and come to nothing.
The shade of that great being answered:

> "If I heard you right, your soul's struck
> by cowardice, weighing you down, turning
> you away from honor's task, you like a beast
> fleeing a mirage. To separate you from your fear
> I'll tell you why I came and what I heard
> when grief for you first traveled me.
> I was among the beings in-between, summoned
> by a lady so blessed and beautiful that I urged:
> 'Command me!' Her eyes outshone the stars;
> and sweetly, quietly, her voice angelic, singularly
> she started to say to me:
>
> > 'O gracious Mantuan being,
> > whose fame still endures in the world, and will
> > to the world's end—my friend, no friend of fortune,
> > on his way's arid shore stumbles and turns
> > around in dread. And from what I've heard about him

> in Heaven, I fear he may already be so lost
> that I've risen too late to help. So hurry
> through the elegance of your speech, support him,
> and by any necessary means; and I'll be comforted.
> I am Beatrice who charges you: Go;
> I come from the place where I want to return;
> love which moved me makes me speak.
> When I'm with my Lord, I'll often praise you.'

Then she was quiet and I began:

> 'O virtuous lady, through you only is humankind
> pre-eminent within the heavens' smallest circle;
> your command upraises me so that obeying you now's
> already too late: just disclose your will
> to me. But tell me why you don't shield yourself
> against the descent into this central deep from the ample
> sphere you burn for.'

She answered me:

> 'Why am I not afraid to come to this place?
> Because you yearn to know
> I will tell you, without an extra word:
> only what causes us pain
> should frighten us, nothing else, nothing
> else to make us afraid. I am so made by God, his
> mercy, no wretchedness here can touch me
> nor can any of these fires' shooting flames have me.
> A gentle lady in Heaven so laments the barred
> path of the friend I send you to that she's facing
> down the high exacting fiat.

This lady called to Lucy and said:

        'Your man of faith
needs you now, to you I commend him.'
Lucy, foe of all cruel beings, rose and came
to where I was sitting near ancient Rachel.
Lucy said, 'Beatrice, God's true laud, do
help this being who so loved you that he quit
the mean horde. Do you hear the distress in his cry?
Don't you see, near that swollen river barred from the sea,
death engage him?'
                      In the wake of these words,
from my hallowed seat I hurried down like a being
on earth who swiftly seeks his good and flees the spring
of pain—trusting in the decency of your words,
which honors both you and your hearers.'

After talking to me like that Beatrice fixed me all the more,
in tears; her eyes shone: I felt an even greater
urgency and so as she wanted I came to you.
                           I saved you
from the she-wolf blocking your way
to the short path of the beautiful mountain.
So? Why, why delay? Why irrigate your cowardice?
Where are your daring and your sincerity?
Consider those three blessed women in Heaven's court
who care for you; consider how much good inheres
in my promise to you."

As little flowers, hunched and closed in night's
chill, unfold on their stems in the bright sun,
that's how it was with me, so weary—and freed by
the run of courage within my heart I began:

        "O praise to her, the compassionate one!
        And to you whose high civility prompted your submission
        to her true words! Through *yours* my heart is moved
        with desire for the journey; I return to my first intent.
        Go now, we are one will—you: guide, lord, master."

That's how I spoke to him; when he'd moved on
I went in to the deep and savage path.

that before 1648 a substantial settlement had sprung up on the east side of the river.

In a brief submitted by Brant van Slichtenhorst in 1656 to the district court of the Veluwe, in the Netherlands, the statement is made that on his arrival in the colony, in March 1648, there were, besides the patroon's trading house, but three houses standing near the fort; that in August of the same year eight houses had been built; and that at the end of his administration, in 1652, there was a settlement of about one hundred houses. Considering these statements in connection with various allusions to building operations which occur in the records, it seems that between 1648 and 1652, apparently at Van Slichtenhorst's initiative and probably for reasons of greater safety and convenience, the settlers on the east side of the river gradually removed to the west side, in the immediate vicinity of the fort.

The erection of these new houses soon attracted the attention of Director Stuyvesant, who objected to their location on the ground that they endangered the security of the fort. Claiming that the jurisdiction of the fort included all territory within range of cannon shot, reckoned at 600 geometrical paces of 5 feet to the pace, he ordered the destruction of all buildings within a radius corresponding to this range, a distance which was afterwards estimated at 150 rods. The order called forth a vigorous protest from Van Slichtenhorst, who regarded it as an invasion of the patroon's rights and who proceeded with the erection of the buildings. A bitter controversy ensued, in the course of which various charges were brought against Van Slichtenhorst, who was summoned to appear at the Manhatans and was there thrown into prison and detained for four months. At length, in the spring of 1652, being determined to settle his dispute with Van Slichtenhorst, Director Stuyvesant repaired to Fort Orange and there issued his proclamation erecting a court for Fort Orange and the village of Beverwyck, apart from and independent of that of the colony of Rensselaerswyck.

The newly created court, which was termed a *Kleine Banck van Justitie*, an inferior bench of judicature, was a court for the head]. The remaining two hogsheads, which spoiled, he tried to improve with the help of Mr van Hamel, as the plaintiff afterwards also sought to do with the said Hamel's help.

The parties having been heard, the court orders the plaintiff to take back the wine in question. In regard to the damage, [309] the plaintiff's demand is denied and the defendant is discharged.

Jochim, the baker, requests the court to grant him a place for a garden.

The court will take the request under advisement and after inspection of the place requested, accommodate the said Jochim in all fairness.

The Honorable Anderies Herbertsen, magistrate, has declared before the court that the 27th of this month a Maquaes savage came quite drunk into his house and after committing many acts of violence left some goods in his house. Coming the other day to the said house to fetch his goods, he declared to the deponent that the wine which made him drunk was bought by three squas from Barent Pietersen, the miller.

November 7, Anno 1656

Ordinary session. Present: La Montagne, commissary; Rutgher Jacobsz:, Andries Harperss:, Jacob Schermerhooren and Philip Pieterss:, magistrates.

Juffrouw Johanna t'Hulter, plaintiff, against Tomas Clabbort, defendant.

The plaintiff demands payment of a certain account delivered to the defendant.

The defendant maintains that he satisfied her by means of a counter-claim delivered to the plaintiff.

The parties having been heard, it is ordered by the court that the plaintiff shall within the space of fourteen days state her objections to the defendant's account.

[310] Juffrouw t'Hullert,[65] plaintiff, against Govert Hendericksen, defendant.

---

[65] Madam Johanna de Hulter.

The defendant failing to appear, default is taken against him. N. B. Also default for the second and third times.

Harmen Jacobsen, plaintiff, against Jan Roeloffsen, Gerrit Hendericksen and Huybert Janssen, defendants.

The court orders the defendant, Huybert Janssen, to pay the admitted debt within the space of three months and orders default to be entered against Jan Roeloffsen and Gerrit Hendericksen.

Arent vanden Berch, plaintiff, against Henderick Gerritsen, defendant.

The defendant failing to appear, default is taken against him.

Cornelis Teunissen, plaintiff, in a case of slander against Abraham Stevensen Crawaet, defendant.

The defendant failing to appear, default is taken against him.

The officer, in a case of slander and insolence, plaintiff, against Tomas Chambert, *alias* Clabbort.

The plaintiff demands reparation for abusive remarks made in his presence and that of the entire court about the honorable directors, the director general and council and the entire court on the 6th of November last in the house of Willem Freedericksen Bout, where the [311] said court and the surveyors were met to decide some question regarding the survey.

The defendant excuses himself on the ground that he was drunk and does not know what he said or did, saying that he is sorry that he used offensive language to his superior authorities. He promises not to do it again and declares that he is ready to undergo such punishment as he deserves in case he should repeat the offense, craving pardon for the fault committed.

The court, observing the defendant's sorrow and his promises, and considering the condition he was in when he uttered the said abusive remarks, excuses him for the present from undergoing the merited punishment and, preferring leniency to rigor, condemn the defendant to pay a fine of one hundred and fifty guilders, to be paid within the space of six weeks.

N. B. the time will expire on the 20th of December.

November 22, Anno 1656

Ordinary session held in Fort Orange. Present: Rutgher Jacobss:, Andries Harperss:, Jacob Schermerhooren and Philippe Pieterss:, magistrates.

Frans Barentsen Pastoor, plaintiff, against Abraham Pietersen Vosborch, defendant.

The plaintiff demands payment of a balance of twenty-seven pieces of beaver at fl. 10 apiece, in seawan, which the defendant paid him in seawan at fl. 8 apiece, so that there is still due him fl. 54.

[312] The defendant maintains that he paid the twenty-seven beavers in full in seawan, at fl. 8 apiece.

The parties having been heard, the defendant is ordered to pay the plaintiff the sum of fl. 54 in seawan.

Frans Barentsen Pastoor, plaintiff, against Jan van Breemen, defendant.

The defendant failing to appear, default is taken against him.

Frans Barentsen Pastoor, plaintiff, against Jan Martensen, *alias* the weaver, defendant.

The defendant failing to appear, default is taken against him.

Lowies Cobus, as attorney, plaintiff, against Frans Barentsen Pastoor, defendant.

The plaintiff says that he had ten beavers attached in the hands of the defendant, which ten beavers the defendant paid in spite of the attachment.

The defendant says that he paid them by order of the court.

The plaintiff asks adjournment until the next court day, in order to have Pieter Brouwer subpoenaed.

The court consents to the adjournment.

Fop Barentsen, plaintiff, against Cornelis Vos, defendant.

The plaintiff demands payment of one hundred and fifty guilders loaned by him to the defendant some weeks ago.

The defendant denies that he owes the plaintiff any money.

[313] The court orders the plaintiff to prove the alleged debt on the next court day by written contract or testimony of witnesses.

November 28, Anno 1656

Ordinary session held in Fort Orange. Present: **R**utgher Jacobs:, Andries Harpertss:, Jacob Schermerhooren and Philippe Pieterss:, magistrates.

Juffrouw de Hulter, plaintiff, against Jan Gouw.

The plaintiff demands payment for 1200 tiles, amounting to seven and a half beavers.

The defendant denies that he owes the plaintiff the sum of fl. 64.

The parties having been heard, the defendant is ordered by the court to pay the plaintiff the sum of fl. 64 in beavers within the space of six weeks.

Cornelis Cornelissen, the younger, plaintiff, against Claes Vylens, defendant.

The defendant failing to appear, default is taken against him.

Foppe Barens, plaintiff, against Cornelis Vos, defendant.

The plaintiff, pursuant to the order of the court of the 22 of November last, produces Marcelus Janssen and Harmen Bastiaensen, as witnesses, who, appearing, testify that being requested by the parties to adjust their differences, the defendant's wife said that she would not speak of anything that happened before, as a result of which they, [314] the deponents, parted without having accomplished anything.

The court orders that a copy of the testimony of the witnesses shall be delivered to the defendant for his consideration and if he has any objections to make he is to submit them on the next court day.

Arent van den Berch, plaintiff, against Henderick Gerritsen, defendant.

The parties having been heard, the defendant is ordered to pay 3 beavers when called upon to do so.

The following persons are summoned to appear on account of their being found in the taverns after the ringing of the bell, contrary to the ordinance:

Harmen Jacobsen Bambus, tavernkeeper. **Paid.**
Jan Gauw } **Default.**
Harmen, the carpenter }
Jan Eeckelen. **Paid.**
Teunis Jacobsen. **Default.**
Albert, the carpenter, tavernkeeper. **Paid.**
Geurt Hendericksz } **Default.**
Gerrit Viesbeeck }
Daniel, the baker. **Paid.**
Henderick *Clootendraeyer* (ball turner) }
Henderick, the tailor, *alias* " Cordiael " } **Default**
Henderick, *alias* the " Styve Snyder " (stiff tailor) }

Jacob Janssen van Noortstrant requests the court to be appointed gager of the casks.

The court grants the request.

[315][66] Ordinary session held in Fort Orange on the 5th of December Anno 1656.

Present: Andries Harpartss:, Jacob Schermerhooren and Philippe Pieterss:, magistrates.

Anderies Herbertsen, as attorney of Goosen Gerritsen, plaintiff, against Claes Teunissen, defendant.

The plaintiff demands payment of a note of fl. 848:—

The defendant admits that he owes a certain balance of account and offers to pay it with his house, requesting that the plaintiff show his power of attorney.

The court orders the plaintiff to show his power of attorney on the next court day.

[316] Anderies Herbertsen, plaintiff in a case of slander, against the wife of Henderick, the baker, defendant.

The plaintiff says and complains that the defendant in his absence has called him a double thief who stole her meat out

---
[66] The upper half of the page is blank.

of the tub and her firewood out of her house, which he offers to prove.

The defendant denies having made such accusations, but admits that she said that the plaintiff as her accuser has been the cause of her husband being obliged to pay a fine of fl. 68, as a result of which they had to go without meat and wood.

The parties having been heard, the court orders the plaintiff to furnish the defendant with a copy of his complaint, to which she is to make answer on the next court day.

Jacob Schermerhoorn, plaintiff, against Christoffel Davids, defendant.

The plaintiff demands payment of 14 schepels of maize, being the balance of a note executed more than 10 years ago.

The defendant denies that he owes the amount, but declares that he is satisfied to pay it if the plaintiff swears to it.

The plaintiff having taken the oath, the court orders the defendant to pay the plaintiff two beavers in specie and 10 stivers in seawan.

Claes Hendericksz, plaintiff, against Gerrit Slechtenhorst, defendant.

The plaintiff demands the defendant's reasons for forbidding him to build on his own ground.

[317] The defendant says that the ground on which the plaintiff was busy building, belongs to him as lessee and he maintains that no one has a right to build thereon without his consent during the term of his lease.

The plaintiff exhibits a lease in the defendant's own handwriting, in the margin of which was written that the plaintiff was to have the use of the yard at present in controversy.

The defendant maintains that such use was granted to the plaintiff only to keep his woodpile there and to use the ground for bleaching purposes, offering to prove the same.

The parties having been heard, the court orders the defendant to prove on the next court day that he has granted the use of the yard to the plaintiff only for the purpose of piling up wood and of bleaching there.

Pieter Loockermans, plaintiff, against Matteus Abrahams, defendant.

The plaintiff demands payment of three and a half beavers.

The defendant admits the debt and offers to pay, provided that the three beavers in the hands of Jan Gauw, which the plaintiff has caused to be attached, shall be left at his disposal.

The court orders the defendant to pay the plaintiff the three and a half beavers. Meanwhile, the attachment of the three beavers is sustained.

Matteus Abrahamsen, plaintiff, against Jan Gauw, defendant.

The defendant failing to appear, default is taken against him.

[318] Foppe Barentsen, plaintiff, against Cornelis Vos, defendant.

The defendant submits his defense in writing, of which a copy is asked by the plaintiff.

The court orders the defendant to furnish the plaintiff with a copy of his defense, to which he is to file his answer on the next court day.

Albert Gysbertsen, wheelwright, requests a certain lot for a garden.

The court will first inspect the place so as to accommodate the petitioner according to its location.

Arent van Curler, having power of attorney from Adriaen Janssen from Leyden, tavernkeeper in the colony of Renselaerswyck, plaintiff, against Marcelus Janssen, formerly farmer of the excise on wine, beer and liquor sold by the tavernkeepers of Fort Orange, the village of Beverwyck and the dependencies thereof, defendant.

The plaintiff demands the return of an anker of brandy which the defendant about 13 months ago, on his own authority and without the knowledge of and consent of the officer of Fort Orange and the village of Beverwyck, unlawfully seized on the public street and highway and appropriated to himself, for which aforesaid [319] anker of brandy, the principal duly ordered and directed his servant to obtain a retail certificate from the aforesaid farmer, as was actually requested, according to the affidavit filed herewith. The plaintiff requests therefore that the defendant be ordered to restore the aforesaid anker of brandy without loss or damage, all according to law.

Was signed: Arent van Curler.

The defendant requests a copy of the plaintiff's demand.

The court orders that a copy of the plaintiff's demands shall be delivered to the defendant.

December 12, Anno 1656

Ordinary session held in Fort Orange

Harmen Jacobsen, plaintiff, against Pieter Stevensen, defendant.

The plaintiff demands payment of fl.30, which the defendant owes.

The defendant admits that he owes fl.23:12, and no more.

The court orders the defendant to pay the acknowledged sum of fl.23:12.

Leendert Philipsen, plaintiff, against Tierck Claessen, defendant.

[320] The plaintiff says that the defendant, having hired a house from him, has without his knowledge sublet it to some one else and requests that the rent thereof be paid to him.

The defendant agrees to it.

The court orders that the plaintiff shall receive the rent of his own house.

Foppe Barentsen, plaintiff, against Cornelis de Vos, defendant.

The defendant asks for a copy of the plaintiff's demand.

The court orders the plaintiff to furnish the defendant with a copy of his demand, to file his answer thereto on the next court day.

Anderies Herbertsen, plaintiff, against Claes Teunissen, defendant.

The plaintiff exhibits his power of attorney.

The court refers the parties to the previously issued order.

Frans Barentsen Pastoor, plaintiff, against Jan van Bremen and Pieter Bronck, defendants.

The parties failing to appear, the second default is taken against Jan van Bremen and the first default against Pieter Bronck.

Claes Hendericksen, plaintiff, against Gerrit Slechtenhorst, defendant.

The defendant produces Jan de Ret [67] as a witness, who testifies that he was present when the copy [321] of the lease between the parties was changed or added to and that he heard the defendant simply grant the use of the yard in question to the plaintiff, but that he did not hear him give any consent to build thereon.

---

[67] Jan Dareth.

Finis

INDEX

Abeel, Stoffel Jansen, *see* Jansen, Stoffel
Abrahams, Matteus, 305
Adriaensen, Jacob, wheelwright, lot, 18, 187; to finish wagon, 72; house sold to Cornelis Segersen, 98, 137, 275, 276; to testify in court, 153, 156; attachment of money due to, 242; money of, paid to Rutger Jacobsen, 286;
    sues Van Bremen, 96; Van Loosdrecht, 153, 165, 169;
    sued for wages, 133, 134; for debt, 135, 136, 137; by Ryverdingh, 259
Adriaensen, Jan, 155
Adriaensen, Pieter, permission to tap, 45; fined for unlawful tapping, 51; sues Cornelis Vos, 121; petition regarding attachment of beer, 202;
    sued for wages, 122, 123; for debt, 294
Adriaensen, Rut, *see* Arentsen, Rutger
Aelbrechts, Femmitge, *see* Alberts, Femmetgen
Aeltgie (Fair Alida), 262, 284. *See also* Jans, Aelgen
Aertsen, Aert, 70
Aertsen, Wouter, *see* Van Putten, Wouter Aertsen
Albert, the carpenter, *see* Gerritsen, Albert
Alberts (Aelbrechts), Femmetgen, examination of, 26; sued for debt, 73, 219; widow of Hendrick Jansen Westerkamp, 182; sues De Wolff and Slichtenhorst, 214, 215, 217; called Geverts, 219; money belonging to, 243; married to Michiel Antonisz, 282; marriage annulled, 283
Albertsen (Aelbertsen), Barent, 185, 272

Albertsen, Willem, complaints against by De Hooges, 36, 43; fighting, 36, 37; settlement with Dyckman, 136; paid for lease of yacht, 140;
    sues Clomp 35; Bronck, 141; Gerbertsen, 168, 171;
    sued for beavers, 31; by Dirck Nes, 32; for stealing a cheese, 36; by Schuyler, for contempt of court, 66, 67; for debt, 74, 108, 130, 140; for return of a jack, 172
Allerton, Isaac, 147
Andriessen (Bradt), Albert, sues Herpertsen, 95, 131; payment to, 131; son-in-law, 136; requests a lot, 185; prosecuted for holding separate divine service and attachment of house rent, 251, 255, 258
Andriessen (Bradt), Arent, oath of burgher, 49; dispute about a gun, 154; loan of money to Director General, 162; testimony, 214, 215, 219
Andriessen (Driess, Van Driest), Hendrick, 20, 140, 298
Andriessen, Luykas, 108
Andryesen, Jan, 190
Antonisen, Michiel, 282, 283
Appel, Adriaen Jansen, *see* Jansen (Appel), Adriaen
Arent the Noorman, *see* Andriesen (Bradt), Arent
Arentsen, Rutger, petition for lot, 16; sues Jacobsen, 54; promise to marry Giertgen Nannix, 57; death, 132; house, 211; settlement of estate, 268
    sued for debt, 53, 71; for slander, 56, 65; for wages, 95, 118; by Bout, 27; by Jansen, 68; by Gerritsen, 85, 93
Ariaen from Alckmaer, *see* Pietersen, Ariaen

Backer, Jacob, 232

Backer, Jochim, *see* Wesselsen, Jochem

Bamboes (Bambus), Herman Jacobsen, prosecuted for violating ordinances, 241, 303; complaints against, for unlawful acts at his tavern, 243, 260, 261, 262, 271; appearance in court, 272;

    sues Margaret Chambers, 275; Jochem Wesselsen, 279;

    sued by De Deckere, 261; for debt, 264, 274, 279

Banker (Bancker), Gerrit, 226, 229, 230, 233, 234

Barentsen (Barens), Foppe, 297, 301, 302, 305, 306

Barentsen, Frans, *see* Pastoor, Frans Barentsen

Barentsen, Jan, 293

Bastiaensen, Harmen, house, 16, 114; misdemeanors, 46, 57; work on Company's house, 47; engaged as surveyor, 79, 187; ordered to pay collector for goods, 84; requests payment of wages, 107; to build bridge, 143; referee, 154, 155; loan of money to Director General, 162; wife Hestor, 210; to be upheld in capacity of surveyor, 217; testimony, 302; prosecuted for violating ordinances, 303;

    sues Sanders, 27; Hendricksen, 53; Jansen, 54; Croon, 72; Adriaensen, 122, 123; Jacobsen, 263;

    sued for receipt for beavers, 31; about a lot, 147, 156

Becker, Jochem, *see* Wesselsen, Jochem

Beeckman, Willem 163

Bembo, Jan, soldier, 84, 142

Bensingh (Bensinck, Bentsingh), Dirck, garden, 21, 64, 157, 158; sale of house and garden, 33; appeal to, 72; purchase of yacht, 93; survey of lot, 117;

Bensingh (Bensinck, Bentsingh), Dirck — *Continued*

    asks for more ground, 131; brother-in-law, 252;

    sues Herpertsen, 58, 65; Ryckertsen, 243;

    sued for abusive language, 130, 276; for canceling purchase of a house, 279

Berck, Willem, 257

Biermans (Bierman), Hendrick, 133, 136, 141

Bogardus, Annetgen, 41, 44, 83, 107, 200

Bont (Bout), Piet, wounded by Jan Gouw, 191; prosecuted by De Deckere, 245; for violence at house of Bamboes, 261, 271; referees to consider case, 277; fined, 280

Boon, Cornelis, 254

Boot, Dirck Claessen, 30

Borremans (Forremans), Frans, 86, 88

Bos, Cornelis Teunissen, *see* Van Westbroeck, Cornelis Teunissen

Boucher, Pierre, 90

Bout, Piet, *see* Bont, Piet

Bout, Willem Fredericksen, bailsman, 40, 46, 71; horse mill, 51, 53, 113; ordered to pay collector for goods, 84; complaints about various actions at his house, 86, 94, 108, 110, 121, 300; request to pay tapsters' excise in lump sum, 97; testimony against Clomp, 107; trade in beer, 138, 142, 143, 148; to build bridge, 143; money due to, 148, 196; sued for sale of horses, 150; loan of money to Director General, 163; appears in court for Stoll, 165; statement on nicknames of houses, 201; wife of, 239; referee, 250;

    prosecuted about lot, 83; for slander and assault, 86; for serving liquor on Sunday, 224;

    sues Arentsen, 27; Jacobsen, 144, 147; Teunissen, 69

Bouts, Geertgen, wife of Willem
    Fredericksen Bout, 220. *See also*
    Nanningh (Nannix), Geertgen
Boutsen, Cors, 184, 185, 186, 195, 201
Bradt, Albert Andriessen, *see* Andriessen, Albert
Bradt, Arent Andriessen, *see* Andriessen, Arent
Brant, Adriaen Claessen, **169**
Brant, Jan Claesen, 48, 51
Brantsen, Evert, 46
Bronck, Pieter, lot, 18; fighting at his house, 56, 86, 108, 118; bailsman, 58; asks for extension of time for building on lots, 133; loan of money to Director General, 163; testimony about Jacob Flodder, 191; enjoined from tapping beer, 219; surety for, 236; mentioned, 94;
    sues Michielsen, 29; van Bremen, 43, 276, 278; Herpertsen, 85, 92; Thomassen, 89; Jansen, 154; Pietersen, 171, **178**; Flodder, 178; Gerritsen, 281; Teunissen, 250, 259; Martensen, 285;
    sued by Joost the baker, 20, 24, 28; for debt, 34, 41, 50, 198, 281; by Jacobsen, 35; about his lot, 83; by Albertsen, 141; about payment for grain, 214, 215, 219; by Pastoor, 307
Brouwer, Jacob de, *see* Gerritsen, Jacob, brewer
Brouwer, Pieter, 301
Bruynen, Pieter, 262
Bruynsen (Brynsen), Auckes (Anker), 133, 263
Buildings, occupied by court, 10

Calendar of the minutes, 11
Canaqueese, an Indian, 91
Carstensen (the Noorman), Carsten, lot, 138, 185, 220; suit for recovery of beavers, 236; wife, 242; sued for debt, **275**

Carstensen (**Cassersen**), Hendrick, 45
Chambers (Clabb**orts**), Margriet, 275
Chambers (Chambre, Clabbort, Chiambers), Thomas, lot, 245; accounts with Slecht, 262; moneys in custody of, 281, 296; mentioned, 106, 226; prosecuted for slanderous remarks about court, 300;
    sues de Forrest, 17; Jacobsen, 224; Jacob Stol, 244; 246; 252;
    sued by Anna de Hulter, 277, 281, 299; for debt, 281
Clabbort, Thomas, *see* Chambers, Thomas
Clabbort, Margriet, *see* Chambers, Margriet
Claes, Marritgen, 133
Claessen, Ariaen, 179, 183, 187, 207
Claessen, Dirrick, *see* Boot, Dirck Claesen
Claessen, Tierck, lot, 264; sues Powell, 253;
    prosecuted for fighting, 245, 247; for being with Lutherans, 247;
    sued by Leendertsen, 254; for debt, 292; for house rent, 306
Clauw, Frans Pietersen, *see* Pietersen, Frans
Cleyn, *see* Kleyn
Clomp (Klomp), Jacob Symonsen, complaint about attachment of money, 94; abusive language, 94, 107, 108, 110; fined, 111; money sent to Director General in sloop of, 162; mentioned, 71, 96, 183, 184; prosecuted for fighting, 21; for selling brandy to savages, 69, 70, 71, 74;
    sues Croon, 29; van Bremen, 73, 101;
    sued for debt, 29, 30; for return of boards, 35; for non-delivery of wheat, 66; about lot, 83; for payment of fine,

Clomp (Klomp), Jacob Symonsen — *Continued*
    85; for wages, 172; for failure to deliver hogs, 183, 184
Clomp, Jan, 29
Clootendraeyer, Hendrick, 303
Cnyver, Claes Thysen, 130
Cobes (Cobus), Ludovicus, asks permission to keep school, 238; attorney for Jan Peeck, 291, 297; sues the wife of Jeles Fonda, 294; sues Frans Barentsen Pastoor, 301. *See also* Jacobussen, Loys
Coenraets, Hans, 242, 250
Coeymans, Barent Pietersen, *see* Pietersen, Barent
Coeymans, Luykas Pietersen, *see* Pietersen, Luykas
Colebrantsen, Pieter, 262
Coninck (Koninck), Thomas, 149
Cornelis, Broer, *see* Teunissen, Cornelis, from Breuckelen
Cornelis, the Swede, 180, 181
Cornelis, Lysbet, 53, 93, 101, 135, 146
Cornelissen, Arent, *see* Vogel, Arent Cornelisen
Cornelissen (Van den Berch, Van den Hoogen Bergh), Claes, 117, 132, 279
Cornelissen, Cornelis, 277, 278, 282
Cornelissen, Cornelis, the younger, 302
Cornelissen, Gysbert, from Breuckelen, 210
Cornelissen, Gysbert, from Weesp, wife, 53, 102; lot, 61, 89, 111; deceased, 89; guardians of children, 146
Cornelissen, Lambert, 69
Cornelissen, Marten, *see* Van Ysselsteyn, Marten Cornelisen
Cornelissen, Pieter, wife of, 183
Cornelissen, Poulus, 279
Cornelissen (Van Voorhout), Seeger, 169, 172
Cornelissen, Teunis, *see* Van Slingerlant, Teunis Cornelisen; Van Vechten, Teunis Cornelisen

Court, jurisdiction, 7, 8–9; buildings occupied by, 10
Court records, handwriting, 12
Cramer, Barent, 50
Croaet (Crabaat, Crowaet), Abraham Stevensen, 118, 183, 184, 191, 300
Croon (Kroon), Claes Cornelissen, 33, 41, 68
Croon (Kroon), Dirck Jansen, money due to, 141; house nicknamed, 200; magistrate, 236; to request contributions for Willem Jurriaensen, 255;
    sues Bastiaensen, 31, 57; Groot, 284;
    sued about axhandle planks, 29; regarding disputed accounts, 72. *See also* Jansen, Dirrick

Daniel, the baker, *see* Rinckhout, Daniel
Daret, Jan, sued by van Aecken, 28, 29, 33; by Jansen, 34; testimony regarding Catelyn Sanders, 231; witness for Gerrit Slichtenhorst, 307
Davidts (Davits, Davitsen), Christoffel, complaints about selling brandy to savages, 71, 88, 106; letter to from Director General, 190; transfer of claim to Pieter Bronck, 281; sued for debt, 292, 296, 304; mentioned, 93
De Deckere, Johannes appointed commissary, 223; salary, request for, 249; to request contributions for Willem Jurriaensen, 255
De Forest (Forrest), Isaack, 17
De Goyer, Eldert, 141
De Graef, Jan, 293
De Hinsse, Surgeon Jacob, 149, 191, 196, 293
De Hooges, Anthony, offensive conduct of Albertsen toward, 36, 43; petition from, 136; referee, 134, 184; lot, 137; garden, 158; charges against Claes Ripsen, 188; state-

De Hooges, Anthony — *Continued*
ment regarding nicknames given to houses, 198; house, 200; mentioned, 78, 159, 193, 205
De Hulter, Johan, servant, 88, 106, 207; house, 109, 113, 114; brings further suit, 116; sues Albertsen, 172; requests letters of recommendation to the honorable council, 230; widow, 262; mentioned, 131, 190
De Hulter (Thullert), Madam Johanna, agreement with Chambers and Stol about grain, 252; mentioned, 262;
 sues Chambers, 277, 281, 299; Jacobsen, 298; Hendricksen, 299; Gouw, 302
De Karreman, Michiel, 210
De Looper, Jacob, *see* Teunissen, Jacob
De Paus, 168
De Truy, Susanna, 205
De Visscher (Visser), Jan, 52, 58
De Vlamingh, Pieter, 219. *See also* Winnen (Winne), Pieter
De Vos, Andries, lot, 69, 97, 173; request for pasture, 107; garden, 112, 173; attorney for Vosburgh, 155, 173; petition of, 160; summoned to court, 164, 210; requests copy of testimony, 222; judgment against, 224; mentioned, 157, 210; sued by Jacobsen, 225;
 sues Gerritsen and others, 190, 192; Bronck, 281
De Vries, Adriaen Dircksen, 184, 239
De Wever, *see* Martensen, Jan
De Winter, Maximiliaen, 87
De Wit, Tierck Claessen, *see* Claessen, Tierck
De Wolff, Jacob Willemsen, *see* Willemsen, Jacob
Dingeman, Adam, 201
Dirck (Dirrick), Oom, 150, 199
Dircksen, Adriaen, *see* De Vries, Adriaen Dircksen
Dircksen, Jan, *see* Van Bremen, Jan Dircksen

Dircksen (Dirricksen), Theunis, 132, 268
Douw, Volckert Jansen, *see* Jansen, Volckert
Douwesen Gillis, *see* Fonda, Gillis Douwesen
Driesen, Hendrick, *see* Andriessen, Hendrick
Dutch records, act of *1768* providing for translation of, 12
Dyckman, Joannes, on committee to survey lots, 16; on committee to provide for support of church, 28; lot, 61, 196; authorized to inspect houses of tapsters, 81; complaint against, 94; to prepare case, 96; protest against Dominie Schaets' announcement, 99; reads protest regarding Slichtenhorst, 119; cases referred to, 134; to pay Willem Albertsen, 136; to examine accounts of collector, 142; report on lot for Adriaen Jansen, 159; loan of money to Director General, 162; gives presents to Maquas, 171; on committee to confer with Director General, 174; wife, 203, 204, 207, 268, 292; successor as commissary, 223; settlement of Rut Arentsen's estate, 268; mentioned, 60, 62, 102, 106, 127
Dyckmans, Maritge, 250, 275, 278

Eeckelen, Jan, *see* Van Eeckel, Jan Janssen
Eencluys, Hans Jansen, *see* Inckluis, Hans Jansen
Egberts, Egbertjen, 286, 287
Elbertsen, Reyer, 19
Eldertsen (Eldersen), Ysbrant, 211, 292
Evertsen, Jurgen, 86, 88

Fernow, Berthold, 11
Flodder, Jacob Jansen, prosecuted for fighting, 56; fined for not building on lot, 148; complaint against, 191; slanderous words about court, 217, 221; money to be paid to, 221; lot, 264;

Flodder, Jacob Jansen — *Continued*
  sues Bensingh, 93; Margaret Slichtenhorst, 260;
  sued for slander, 25; about sale of horses, 150, 152; for wages, 172, 175; for debt, 178
Floris, Isaack, 239
Fonda, Gillis Douwesen, 70, 294
Forremans, Frans, *see* Borremans, Frans
Fredericksen, Carsten, 195, 295
Fredericksen, Meyndert, 236, 284
Fredericksen, Willem, *see* Bout, Willem Fredericksen

Gabrielsen, Frans, 37, 39, 40
Gansevoort, Harmen Harmensen, 243
Gardenier, Jacob Jansen, *see* Flodder, Jacob
Gauw, Jan, *see* Gouw, Jan
Geraerdy (Gerary), Philip, 32
Gerbertsen, Elbert, prosecuted for fighting, 56, 57; bail for, 58; fined for failure to inclose lot, 148
  sues Clomp, 183, 184; garden, 201;
  sued about sale of horses, 150; for costs of summons, 168, 171
Gerbrantsen, Cornelis, 172
Gerret, the cooper, 41. *See also* Jansen, Gerrit, from Swoll
Gerritsen, Albert, garden, 84;
  prosecuted for fighting, 69; for violating ordinances, 303;
  sues Herpertsen, 85; Arentsen, 93, 95, 118
Gerritsen, Claes, lot and garden, 97, 102; sues van Slichtenhorst, 135, 142, 144; testimony regarding house of Thomas Sanders, 179; accused of giving nicknames to houses, 198, 201; testimony regarding Cornelis Vos, 213; restitution of beavers in his custody, 228;
  sued, about taking grain from a barn, 190; about a wagon, 209, 210

Gerritsen, Ellert, 83
Gerritsen, Goosen, crime against daughter, 37; lot, 51; fined for not building on lot, 83; payment of account for beer, 94; testimony in trial of Jacob Stoll, 105; prosecuted by Dyckman, 107; curator of Arentsen's estate, 132, 268; payment to for nails, 137; palisades inclosing lot, 149; requests permission to form corral for cattle, 154; loan of money to Director General, 163; gives presents to Maquas, 171; referee, 173, 184, 212, 244, 250; testimony on use of a barn, 192; house nicknamed, 199; testimony regarding Catelyn Sanders, 231; magistrate, 269; mentioned, 66, 73, 147;
  sues Arentsen, 53; Herpertsen, 135; Gansevoort, 243; Vosburgh, 274, 278; Pietersen, 291; Davidts, 292; Teunissen, 292, 303; Van Valckenburgh, 292
Gerritsen, Hendrick, prosecuted for drinking after ringing of the bell, 117; fined for not building on lot, 145; garden, 185; house and lot, 211;
  sued by van Hoesen, 284; for slander, 298; by Vandenburgh, 300, 302
Gerritsen, Jacob, carpenter, 57, 108, 130, 281
Gerritsen, Jacob, the brewer, 18
Gerritsen, Wynant, 145, 166
Geverts, Femmetgen Alberts, *see* Alberts, Femmetgen
Glen, Sander Leendertsen, *see* Leendertsen, Sander
Goosens (Goossens), Maria, 223, 247. *See also* Jans, Maria
Gottenborgh, Jan Jansen, *see* Jansen, Jan

Gouw (Gauw, Gou), Jan, sues Jacobsen, 156, 292, 297; testimony regarding fighting at Jochemsen's house, 166; attack on Bout, 191; lot, 220; testimony on fighting at house of Baefge Pieters, 257;
  prosecuted for fighting, 55, 57; for violating ordinances, 303; sued for debt, 153, 247, 274, 302; by Jansen, 235; by Ryverdingh, 239; by Abrahamsen, 305
Greenen Bosch, 7, 220
Groot, Symon, 145, 284
Gysbertsen, Albert, 305

Hansen, Volckert, see Jansen, Volckert
Hap, Jacob Jansen, see Stol, Jacob Jansen
Hap, Willem, see Stol (Hap), Willem
Haps, Geertruy, 280
Harmen, the carpenter, see Bastiaensen, Harmen
Harmensen, Dirckie, 289, 290
Harmensen, Harmen, see Gansevoort, Harmen Harmensen
Hartgers (Hertgers, Harties), Pieter, referee, 27, 93; magistrate, 42, 126, 139, 236; fined for not inclosing garden, 83; sued for payment for goods, 134, 135; money due to, 141, 196; lot, 145, 212, 276; appointed guardian, 146; loan of money to Director General, 163; gives presents to Maquas, 171; conveyance of houses, 197; house nicknamed, 200; bed sold to, 214, 216; appointed treasurer of court, 214, 215; dispute about pint measure, 220; sentence decreed against advice of, 225; sues Bamboes, 264; grant of land to, 255; gift for repairing Jurriaensen's house, 256; surety for payment for blockhouse church, 263; mentioned, 17, 66, 150, 223

Helmensen, Jan (Jan with the beard), 260
Hendrick, alias the "Styve Snyder," 303
Hendrick, the baker, see Hendricksen, Hendrik
Hendrick, the tailor, alias "Cordiael," 303
Hendrick Clootendraeyer (ball turner), 303
Hendricksen, 191, 221
Hendricksen, Claes, loan of money to Director General, 163; surety for Flodder, 172, 175; testimony regarding Maria Jans, 179, 180; lot, 187, 245; house, 197; fined, 242; money in custody of, 242; sues Slichtenhorst, 304, 307;
  sued for house rent, 209; by Swart, 210; for return of beavers, 237
Hendricksen, Cornelis, 53
Hendricksen, Frederick, 291
Hendricksen, Gerrit, 300
Hendricksen, Geurt (Govert), 220, 298, 299, 303
Hendricksen, Hendrik, 278, 285, 303
Hendricksen, Jacob, see Maat, Jacob Hendricksen; Sibbinck, Jacob Hendricksen
Hendricksen, Jan, sued by Dyckman, 117; to build bridge, 143; loan of money to Director General, 162; house, 179, 184; sues van Aecken, 179; sues Jan Baptist van Rensselaer, 244
Hendricksen, Marten, bailsman, 40; sued for debt, 55, 58, 64, 66, 154, 155, 194; complaint about Seeger Cornelisen, 168; to contribute for bridge, 169; mentioned, 17
Herbertsen (Herpertsen), Andries, referee, 18, 64, 102, 209; garden, 95; letter to from members of court, 113; memorandum for, 114; magistrate, 126, 236; dispute with Van Valckenborgh, 136; term of

Herbertsen (Herpertsen), Andries
— *Continued*
    office expired, 139; accounts with Keese Waeye, 156; questioned in court on various matters, 158; loan of money to Director General, 162; gives presents to Maquas, 171; house nicknamed, 199; gift for repairing Jurriaensen house, 256; sentence rendered contrary to his judgment, 281; statement on selling liquor to savages, 299; attorney of Goosen Gerritsen, 303; case of slander, 303; mentioned, 49, 131, 133, 138, 165, 168, 290;
  sues Femmetgen Westerkamp, 182; Claes Teunissen, 306
Herpertsen, Marten, lot, 45, 83; sale of house and garden, 94, 109, 113, 114; complaints by creditors, 137;
  sued for debt, 32, 38, 65, 82, 83, 85, 92, 93, 95, 97, 101, 131, 135, 140, 141, 144, 145, 148, 170; by van Hoesen, 58; by the Visscher, 58; by Bensingh, 58
Hertgers, Pieter, *see* Hartgers, Pieter
Higge (Higgins), Thomas, 29, 30
Hoffmeyer, Willem, summoned to court, 118; fined, 277; punished for selling beer to savages, 288;
  sued by Jansen, 235, 247; by Bamboes, 275; for debt, 278, 279; by Wesselsen, 298
Hollenbeck, C. A., 11
Hoogenboom, Cornelis Pietersen, 293
Houses, nicknames given to, 198–200, 210, 213
Houtewael, Cornelis, 172, 175
Houttum, Willem, 156

Inckluis, (Eencluys), Hans Jansen, 194
Indians, sale of liquors to, 69, 70, 71, 74, 88, 106, 164, 167, 286–91

Jacob, the brewer, *see* Gerritsen, Jacob, brewer
Jacob, the carpenter, *see* Gerritsen, Jacob, carpenter
Jacobs (Jacops), Grietgen, 201, 282
Jacobs, Tryntgen, 168
Jacobs, Wybregh (Brecht), 38, 210
Jacobsen, Abraham, 86, 88, 198
Jacobsen (Jacopsen), Aert, 54
Jacobsen, Andries, 231
Jacobsen, Caspar, 18
Jacobsen, Claes, 68, 185, 213, 215, 263
Jacobsen, Cornelis, 32, 35
Jacobsen, Herman, petition to qualify as beer carrier, 218;
  sues Hendricksen, 209; Wesselsen, 282; Roeloffsen and others, 300; Stevensen, 306;
  sued by Gouw, 292, 297; by Johanna de Hulter, 298
Jacobsen (Jacopsen), Roeloff, sues Gouw, 153; Tryntgen Jacobs, 168; Inckluis, 194; Marten the farmer, 244;
  sued for debt, 94, 95, 133; for house rent, 153; by Gouw, 156
Jacobsen, Rutger, referee, 20, 51, 102, 173, 212; boards belonging to, 35; opinion on tapsters' excise, 44; residence, 48; attorney for Jan van Hoesen, 49, 52, 55; money for, from Clomp, 94; letter to from members of court, 113; horse mill, 113; memorandum for, 114; magistrate, 126, 236; payment for boards, 131; curator of Arentsen's estate, 132, 268; term of office expired, 139; garden, 140, 217; hires yacht, 140; requests permission to form corral for cattle, 154; gives presents to Maquas, 171; charges against Claes Ripsen, 188; house nicknamed, 199; testimony, 226, 231; judgment in favor of, 228; rejects Johan de Deckere's request for

Jacobsen, Rutger — *Continued*
salary, 249; water wheel for a small mill, 255; gift for repairing Jurriaensen's house, 256; money paid to, 285; mentioned, 22, 29, 30, 70, 135, 142, 144, 255, 290;
sues Clomp, 66; Albertsen, 140; Femmetgen Alberts, 219;
sued by Fredericksen, 144, 147; for wages, 267
Jacobsen (Jacopsen), Teunis, 18, 188, 224, 225, 303
Jacobusen, Loys, 205. *See also* Cobes, Ludovicus
Jan de Cuyper, *see* Schut, Jan
Jan, the soldier, *see* Bembo, Jan
Jan, the weaver, *see* Martensen, Jan
Jan with the beard, *see* Helmensen, Jan
Jans, Aelgen, 210. *See also* Aeltgie (Fair Alida)
Jans, Jannitge, 239, 278
Jans, Maria, sale of brandy to savages, 179, 187, 191; sues Croaet, 183, 191; dispute about a water pail, 190; must pay for bed, 214, 216; dispute about a pint measure, 220; ordered to suspend tapping, 221. *See also* Goosens, Maria
Jans, Marritgen, 37. *See also* Ryverdingh, Marriecke
Jans, Volckgen, *see* Jurriaens, Volckgen
Jansen (Appel), Adriaen, from Leyden, marriage, 23, 26; lot, 53, 61, 82, 159; referee, 57, 93; testimony of what occurred at the house of Fredricksen, 108, 110; nominated magistrate, 126; loan of money to Director General, 163; charges against Claes Ripsen, 197; statement regarding nicknames given to houses, 198; ordered to build on lot, 263; fined, 284; dispute about an anker of brandy, 305; mentioned, 107, 205;
sues Westerkamp, 34; Daret, 34;

Jansen (Appel), Adriaen — *Continued*
Bronck, 34; van Valckenburgh, 34; van Bremen, 43
Jansen, Claes, from Baarn, appointed inspector, 122, 154; report, 155; testimony, 219; fined, 260, 261; referee, 263
Jansen, Claes, from Rotterdam, 122, 150, 199
Jansen, Dirck, 16, 17, 54, 66. *See also* Croon, Dirck Jansen
Jansen, Fop, 267
Jansen, Gerrit, from Swoll, house sold by, 101; testimony, 105, 136; magistrate, 126; loan of money to Director General, 162; house nicknamed, 199; mentioned, 131. *See also* Gerrit, the cooper
Jansen, Harman, *see* Van Valckenburgh, Herman Jansen
Jansen, Hendrick, the cowherd, accused of making lampoons, 248, 251; fighting, 254, 257; prosecuted by de Deckere, 254, 260, 272; mentioned, 271
Jansen, Hendrick, *see also* Reur, Hendrick Jansen; Westerkamp, Hendrick Jansen
Jansen, Herman, 184, 186
Jansen, Huybert, *de guyt*, 154, 233, 284, 300
Jansen, Jacob, *see* Flodder, Jacob Jansen; Schermerhoorn, Jacob Jansen; Stol (Hap), Jacob Jansen
Jansen, Jan, sues Albertsen, 31; money due to, 38; power of attorney to Rem Jansen, 82; holds mortgage on house, 116; power of attorney given to, 156; sued for debt, 221. *See also* Van Eeckel, Jan Janssen
Jansen, Juriaen, 223, 224, 266, 271, 293
Jansen, Karsten, 162
Jansen, Laurens, petition, 41; fighting, 75, 96; testimony on sale of brandy to savages, 88; testimony on shooting by Stol, 107, 111; house, 145, 211; mentioned, 83, 106 236

Jansen, Marcelis, servant of Mr de Hulter, 88; complaint of assault, 184, 185, 206; testimony, 106, 213, 214, 215, 219, 302; prosecuted for serving drinks during divine service, 235;
    sues De Paus, 168; Pot, 225; Verwegen, 225; Hendricksen, 242; Rinckhout, 253; Loserik, 268; Adriaensen, 294;
    sued by Herpertsen, 281; by van Curler, 305

Jansen, Michiel, 282

Jansen, Paulus, the Noorman, 239

Jansen, Rem, referee, 27, 29, 93, 184, 209; demands payment of bond, 82; fined, 83; loan of money to Director General, 163; lot, 210; house and lot, 211; sues Willem Hap, 222; mentioned, 96, 284

Jansen, Roeloff, 130

Jansen, Steven, wife, 179, 183, 187, 191, 203, 204, 214, 216, 220, 221, 223; assault on, 207; sued by van Loosdrecht, 209, 254, 259, 275; fighting with Jacob Hendricksen Maat, 221; mentioned, 207, 211, 254;
    sues Hendricksen, 55, 64, 154, 155; Arentsen, 68; Jacobsen, 94, 95; Croaet, 184; Hofmeyer, 235; Jan Jansen, 221; Jacob Teunissen, 246

Jansen (Abeel), Stoffel, carpenter, 97, 150, 166, 263

Jansen (Mingael), Thomas, 61, 72, 159, 163. *See also* Mingael, Tomas Janssen

Jansen (Hansen, Douw), Volckert, to oversee surveying of lots, 16, 48, 51; referee, 18, 22, 52, 93; opinion on tapsters' excise, 44; Becker's attack on, 62; magistrate, 126, 216, 269; sued for debt, 134, 135; money due to, 141; testimony regarding Vosburgh's lot, 159; loan of money to Director General,

Jansen (Hansen, Douw) Volckert—*Continued*
163; gives **presents** to Maquas, 171; house nicknamed, 200; request concerning lot of poorhouse, 216; sentence decreed against advice of, 225, 239; rejects Johan de Deckere's request for salary, 249; grant of land to, 255; gift for repairing Jurriaensen's house, 256; mentioned, 55, 66, 259;
    sues Becker, 23; Bronck, 24, 41, 50; Bamboes, 264

Jeronimus, Geertruy, sued for abusive language and assault, 17, 19, 21, 25; fined, 26; sues Styntgen Laurens and Volckgen Jans, 29, 32; testimony regarding Albertsen, 37; first default entered against her, 149

Jochem, the baker, *see* Wesselsen, Jochem

Jochemsen, Hendrick, garden, 64; sued for debt, 84, 291; summoned to testify, 96; money due to, 141; loan of money to Director General, 162; testimony regarding Stol and Dirck Lammertssen, 166; petition for restitution of money, 218; granted permission for burghers to shoot the target, 220; fined, 241, 247; mentioned, 117, 118, 165, 166, 198; prosecuted for fighting, 75; for smuggling beer, 83

Joost, the baker, *see* Teunissen, Joost

Jurriaen, the glazier, *see* Jansen, Juriaen

Jurriaens (Jans), Volckgen, sues Geertruy Jeronimus, 17, 19, 21, 25; house, 22; sued by Geertruy Jeronimus, 32; payment of money for Jurriaensen, 80; testimony, 142

Jurriaensen (Juryaensen), Willem, sued about lot, 17, 67, 78, 80; house and lot, 19, 47, 49, 52, 55, 62, 191, 199, 210, 238; petition by, 22;

COURT MINUTES, 1652-1656 319

Jurriaensen (Juryaensen), Willem — *Continued*
  garden, 24; contract with van Hoesen, 63, 67, 78; refuses to accept money, 82; testimony, 118; house, contributions requested for repairing roof, 255; mentioned, 252

Karreman, ship, 180
Ketelhuyn, Jochem, 51, 83, 156, 263
Keyser, Adriaen, 75
Kleyn, Elmerhuysen, 72, 84, 164, 167
Kleyn, Uldrick, 182, 184, 186, 187
Knyver, *see* Cnyver
Koninck, *see* Coninck
Kroon, *see* Croon

Labatie (Labite), Jan, referee, 18, 21; to lay out land, 20; resigns as magistrate to live in the colony, 42; garden, 48; pleads cases, 53; house and lot, 56; lot, 61, 69, 187; magistrate, 126; ordered to return lime, 144; loan of money to Director General, 163; mentioned, 60, 65, 141;
  sues Clomp, 29; Westerkamp, 32; Becker, 58, 119; Hap, 59; Pietersen, 144
La Chair, Salomon, 279
Lademaker, *see* Machiel, the lademaker
Lamberts, Annitge, 260, 261
Lambertsen (Lammertsen), Poulus, 235, 260, 261
Lammertsen, Dirck, 165, 166, 167
Lammertsen, Jan, 187
La Montagne, Jan, 75
Laurens, Styntgen, 29, 32
Lauson (Loison), Jean de, governor of Canada, 90
Leen, Symon, 226
Leendertsen, Gabriel, 82, 141, 145
Leendertsen, Paulus, 60
Leendertsen (Glen), Sander, negress, 16, 24, 27; lot, 56, 112, 113, 212, 276; must pay fees, 59; to collect tax, 77, 111; magistrate, 126, 139, 269; referee, 140; money due to, 141; to build bridge, 143; gives presents to Maquas, 171; conveyance of houses, 197; wife, 231; sues Claesen, 254; gift for repairing Jurriaensen's house, 256; surety bond, 264; payment of money to court, 285; mentioned, 247;

Leendertsen (Glen), Sander — *Continued*
  sued for slander, 16; about sale of horses, 150
Liberis, Catharina, 172
Loison, Johan de, *see* Lauson, Jean de
Loockermans, Pieter, 162, 237, 297, 305
Loosdrecht, Jacob, *see* Van Loosdrecht, Jacob Hendricksen Maat
Loserik, Jacob, *see* Van Loosdrecht, Jacob Hendricksen Maat
Lot, Pieter, 145, 158
Lourensen, Lourens, 133, 148
Luyersen (Van Kuyckendall), Jacob, house and garden, 26; complaint about negress, 27; sued for messenger fees, 59; prosecuted for abusive language and assault, 76, 83, 108, 134; must pay treasurers, 130; must file answer to complaint, 131; pardoned, 134; to pay fine, 134; mentioned, 145, 180
  sues Leendertsen, 16; Cathalina Sanders, 24; Flodder, 25

Maat (Maet), Jacob Hendricksen, farmer of the excise, 176; requests that burghers obtain certificate for beer, 176-77; summoned to testify, 179; payment for excise on wine and beer, 195, 222; charges against, 201; attachment of beer, 202; testimony, 204; judgment against, 211; fighting, 211, 221;
  sues Bronck, 198; Jansen, 209. *See also* Van Loosdrecht, Jacob Hendricksen Maat

Macheck Sipoeti (Indian), 290
Machiel, the lademaker, 41, 44, 83
Machielsen, Jan, see Michielsen, Jan
Maerten, the farmer, see Van Ysselsteyn, Marten Cornelisen
Maertens, Poulus, 247
Marcelis, Hendrick, 108
Marten, Swager, see Ottsen (Ottensen), Martin
Marten, the mason, see Herpertsen, Marten
Martensen (Van Alstyne), Jan, 48, 261, 272, 285, 301
Marttensen, Marten, 73
Megapolensis, Johannes, 33, 44, 185
Melius, Wheeler B., 11
Meussen (Messen), Pieter, 297
Meyndert, the smith, see Fredericksen, Meyndert
Meyndertsen, Carsten, 195
Michielsen (Machielsen), Jan, complaint about negress, 27; testimony at trial of Jacob Stol, 105; to build bridge, 143; mentioned, 31;
    sues Leendertsen, 16; Cathalina Sanders, 20, 24; Albertsen, 36;
    sued by Bronck, 29, 72; for messenger fees, 59; for debt, 282
Mingael, Tomas Janssen, 297. See also Jansen, Thomas

Nanningh (Nannix), Geertgen, 57, 213, 214, 237, 239. See also Bouts, Geertgen
Nes, Dirck, see Van Nes, Dirck
Nicknames given to houses, 198–200
Nolden (Nolding), Evert, 43, 44

Otterspoor, Aert, 190
Ottsen (Ottensen), Marten, 74, 180

Pastoor, Frans Barentsen, excused from paying fine, 67; magistrate, 126, 139, 223, 269; loan of money to Director General, 163; gives presents to Maquas, 171; lot, 212; surety for Pieter

Pastoor, Frans Barentsen — Continued
    Bronck, 235; opinion on granting a lot, 245; asks for relief from certain duties, 245; to request contributions for Willem Jurriaensen, 255; referee, 277; mentioned, 276, 278;
    sues Vosburgh, 247, 250, 253, 297, 301; Loserick, 268, 272; van Bremen, 301, 307; Martensen, 301; Vos, 301; Bronck, 307
Paulw, Tomas, see Powell, Thomas
Pearson, Jonathan, 11–12
Peeck, Jan, 145, 275, 291, 297
Pels, Evert, boards delivered by, 149; sued for debt, 155; petition of, 174; money due from van Bremen, 196, 219; wounding of, 210;
    sues Arentsen, 68, 71; van Hoesen, 154; Bronck, 214, 215, 219
Philipsen, Leendert, 140, 147, 156, 292, 306
Pieter, the baker, 293
Pieters, Baeffgen, 190, 257, 261, 284
Pieters, Geertruyt, 173, 176
Pietersen, Abram, see Vosburgh, Abraham Pietersen
Pietersen, Ariaen, 21, 64
Pietersen (Coeymans), Barent, 299
Pietersen, Cornelis, 190, 192. See also Hoogenboom, Cornelis Pietersen
Pietersen (Clauw), Frans, 260
Pietersen, Gillis, garden, 133, 145; sale of house, 144; referee, 184; testimony regarding a fight, 184, 185; sued for debt, 291
Pietersen (Coeymans), Luykas, fined for not building on lot, 145, 168; prosecuted by Dyckman, 157; garden, 158, 174; sued for debt, 171, 178; complaints against of violence, 184, 186; not guilty of charges, 195
Pietersen, Philip, see Schuyler, Philip Pietersen
Pietersen, Ryndert, 219

Poest, Jan Barentsen sues Marten Hendricksen. 64, 66; fencing off lot, 111; farm, 150, 190, 192; mentioned, 192. *See also* Wemp, Jan Barentsen
Pot (Pott), Cornelis, 179, 225
Poulus, the Noorman, *see* Jansen, Paulus
Poulussen, Gommer, 294
Powell (Paulw, Paul), Thomas, testimony, 226, 242; petition of, 229; prosecuted by de Deckere, 250, 277, 280; sued by Claesen, 253; sues Claesen, 292; mentioned, 229, 234, 241
Pries, Evert, 297
Prins, Willem Jansen, 108

Quick, Jacob Teunissen, *see* Teunissen, Jacob

Rensselaerswyck, court of, 9; consolidated with court of Fort Orange, 9
Reur, Hendrick Jansen, 203
Rinckhout (Ringhaut), Daniel, prosecuted for violating ordinances, 251, 277; petition, 229; judgment against, 277; sues Teunissen, 284; summoned to court, 303;
  sued about grain measures, 175; for payment of excise, 253; by Bamboes 275, 279
Ripsen (Rips, Ribsen), Claes, 68, 188, 197, 260, 291
Roelofsen, Jan, testimony regarding Jacob Stol, 109; fined for not building on lot, 153; appointed surveyor, 187; to build the block-house church, 263; prosecuted by de Deckere, 273; mentioned, 271;
  sued by Bamboes, 272; by Jacobsen, 300
Rosekrans, Lysbet, 56, 65
Rotterdam, Claes, *see* Jansen, Claes, from Rotterdam
Rutgertsen, Ryck, 192

Ryckertsen, Michiel, 145, 243
Ryverdingh, Marriecke, 23, 26. *See also* Jans, Marritgen
Ryverdingh (Reverdingh, Ruyverdingh), Pieter, fees, 17, 30; lot, 61; offers money to Jurriaensen, 80, 82; certificate of delivery of beer and wine, to give, 80, 97; residence, 87; to make up accounts of persons drowned, 94; accounts, 142, 176; money paid to, 237; mentioned, 42, 52, 60, 84, 85;
  sues Luyersen and Michielsen, 59; Jansen, 233; Gouw, 239; Jacob Teunissen, 246; Adriaensen, 259; Jan Schut, 275; Bastiaensen, 279

Sanders (Sandertsen), Cathalina, 20, 24, 231
Sanders (Sanderts), Thomas, garden, 65; unable to pay assessment, 119; testimony regarding Stol and Dirck Lammertsen, 166; house, 179, 184; mentioned, 166;
  sued by Bastiaensen, 27; for debt, 147
Schaets, Rev. Gideon, lot, 61; garden, 64; announcement from pulpit regarding Van Slichtenhorst, 99, 120, 124; charges against Claes Ripsen, 188, 197; surety for Slichtenhorst, 243; requests money for Schrick, 243; mentioned, 60, 66
Schapenbout, Arent, 58
Schellinger, Jan Tjebkens, 136
Schermerhoorn (Schermerhoren), Jacob Jansen, insult to officials, 20; lot, 53; garden, 64, 67, 107, 112, 157, 158; judgment against, 101; to lay out lots, 108, 131, 133, 150; magistrate, 126, 269; referee, 140; appointed guardian, 146; report on lot for Adriaen Jansen, 159; loan of money to Director General, 162; gives

Schermerhoorn (Schermerhoren), Jacob Jansen — *Continued*
presents to Maquas, 171; money paid to, 176; testimonial to, 177; gone to Holland, 177, 216; mentioned, 164; sues Herpertsen, 85, 93; Adriaensen, 135; Loserik, 254, 259; Davidts, 304

Schools, 238

Schrick, Paulus, 73, 243

Schut (de Cuyper), Jan, 275

Schut, Willem Jansen, 194, 213, 215, 241

Schuyler (Schuler, Scheuler, Schuldert), Philip Pietersen, cases referred to, 29, 244; lot, 33, 45, 131, 276; sues Albertsen, 66, 67; house nicknamed, 199; interest in a drag net, 220; testimony, 226, 231; surety bond, 264; magistrate, 269

Segertsen, Cornelis, island of, 24; house sold to, 98, 134, 135, 137; claim against Jacob Adriaensen, 137; appointed guardian, 146; request for woodland, 150; sued for debt, 275

Segertsen, Gerrit, 176, 185

Sibbinck, Jacob Hendricksen, 133, 134, 145

Sille, Nicasius de, 123

Slecht, Cornelis Barentsen, 262

Slichtenhorst, Brant, *see* Van Slichtenhorst, Brant Aertsen

Slichtenhorst, Gerrit, sale of brandy to savages, 164, 167; dispute about chest, 214, 215; fighting, 227, 229; prosecuted for fighting, 234, 237, 238; surety for, 243;
sued for debt, 243; about lease of yard, 304, 307

Slichtenhorst (Slechtenhorst), Margariet, 260

Slingerlant, Teunis, *see* Van Slingerlant, Teunis Cornelisen

Smit, Jan, 55, 57

Staets, Abraham, cases referred to, 21, 52; lot, 48, 61; to collect tax,

Staets, Abraham — *Continued*
77, 111; magistrate, 126; loan of money to Director General, 162; to present powder to Indians, 175; payment of money to court, 285; mentioned, 22, 55, 60, 61

Stevensen, Abraham, *see* Croaet, Abraham Stevensen

Stevensen, Pieter, 306

Stiggery, Stick, an Indian, 90

Stoffel, the carpenter, *see* Jansen (Abeel), Stoffel

Stoffelsen, Reyer, 291, 292

Stol (Hap), Jacob Jansen, abusive words against magistrates, 26, 27; fighting, 59, 96; testimony on shooting by, 103, 107, 109, 111; ordered to present answer to charges, 119; money due to, 148; horses sold to, 150; house, 197; requests permission to purchase land, 230; prosecuted for fighting, 238; fined, 238; appeal from sentence, 239; sued by Chambers, 244, 246, 252; not punished for beating wife, 248; moneys in the custody of, 296; mentioned, 45, 52, 93, 198

Stol (Hap), Willem Jansen, lot, 48, 157, 187; fighting, 165, 166, 167; testimony, 213, 215, 219; ordered to pay for house, 222; taken to guard house, 252;
prosecuted, for drinking during service, 235; by de Deckere, 254, 258, 261;
sued by Bamboes, 279; by Jacobsen, 282

Stuyvesant, Peter, 7, 8, 13, 44, 270

Swager, Marten, *see* Ottsen (Ottensen), Marten

Swart, Gerrit, 120, 210

Symants, Styntge, 19

Symon, the baker, *see* Volckertsen, Symon

Symonsen, Arien, 274

Tappen, Juriaen Teunissen, *see* Teunissen, Juriaen

COURT MINUTES, 1652-1656   323

Teller (Teljer, Tellier), Willem, complaint against, 217; testimony, 226; fighting, 247; to take up monthly collection, 245;
  prosecuted for fighting, 244; for encroachments on public road and slander, 266, 272, 273, 280
Tempelier, Theunis, 218
Ten Haer, Mariken, 73
Tesselaer, Evert, 32, 134, 135
Teunissen, Claes, 250, 259, 292, 303, 306
Teunissen (Theunesen), Cornelis, from Breuckelen, 42, 175
Teunissen, Cornelis, *see also* Van Westbroeck, Cornelis Teunissen
Teunissen (Theunisen), Jacob, 71, 226, 246
Teunissen (Theunissen), Joost, 20, 28, 36, 41, 43, 50
Teunissen (Tappan, Theunissen), Juriaen, denies charges against, 20; sued for debt, 69, 284; fighting at house of, 117, 132; sues Baefge Pieters, 284
Teunissen (Theunissen), Pieter, 172
Theunisen, *see* Teunissen
Thomassen, Cornelis, 95
Thomassen, Frans, 169
Thomassen (Witbeck), Jan, petition, 41; magistrate, 108, 126; loan of money to Director General, 163; gives presents to Maquas, 171; house nicknamed, 199; attorney for Wemp, 210; lot, 212; referee, 253, 254; grant of land to, 255; gift for repairing Jurriaensen's house, 256; ordered to build on lot, 263; examination of an Indian, 290; mentioned, 17, 108, 138;
  sues Albertsen, 130; Schut, 194, 213, 215; Bamboes, 264
Thomassen, Poulus, 89
Thullert, Johanna, *see* De Hulter, Madam Johanna
Thysen, Claes, 163
Thysen, Jacques, 69, 196. *See also* Vander Heyden, Jacob Thysen

Uylenspiegel, Claes, 278, 282

Van Aecken, Jan, sued by Hendricksen, 179; house, 184; house nicknamed, 199; dispute about a chest, 297; mentioned, 147;
  sues Daret, 28, 29, 33; Meyndertsen, 195; Fredericksen, 195
Van Alckmaer, Ariaen, *see* Pietersen, Ariaen
Van Alstyne, Jan Martensen, *see* Martensen, Jan
Van Bremen, Jan Dircksen, indebtedness, 28, 41, 196; testimony regarding Clomp, 70; attachment of money in hands of, 94, 214, 215, 219; summons to court, 219; prosecuted for various offenses, 96; by de Deckere, 245; for wounding Hans Vos, 248; mentioned, 29; sued for debt, 43, 50, 70, 73, 101; for delivery of a hog, 70; for failure to haul logs, 246; by Bronck, 276, 278; by Pastoor, 301, 307
Van Breuckelen, Cornelis Theunesen, *see* Teunissen, Cornelis
Van Couwenhoven, Jacob, 279
Van Curler, Arent, 134, 305
Van den Berch, Claes Cornelissen, *see* Cornelissen, Claes
Van den Bergh (Berch), Arent, 154, 300, 302
Van den Hoogen Bergh, Claes, *see* Cornelissen, Claes
Vander Donck, Adriaen, 193
Vander Heyden, Jacob Thysen, 163. *See also* Thysen, Jacques
Van Driest, Hendrick, *see* Andriessen, Hendrick
Van Duynkercken, Adriaen Jansen, *see* Jansen, Adriaen
Van Eeckel (Ekel, Eeckelen), Jan Janssen, 291, 296, 298, 303
Van Geel, Maximiliaen, 60
Van Groenwout, Juriaen Jansen, *see* Jansen, Juriaen

Van Hamel, Dirk, 239, 299
Van Hoesen (Hoesem, Housen), Jan Franssen, lot and garden, 18, 24, 49, 52, 55, 62, 191, 272; wife, 19, 21, 22, 80, 142; house, 47; contract with Jurriaensen, 63, 67, 78; loan of money to Director General, 162; request concerning Jurriaensen's house, 199, 210; gift for repairing Jurriaensen's house, 256; mentioned, 143, 165;
   sues Jurriaensen, 17, 78, 80; Becker, 55; Herpertsen, 58, 144; Gerritsen, 284;
   sued about house, 47; by Becker, 65; for debt, 154; by de Deckere, 245
Van Ilpendam, Adriaen Jansen, requests promotion to office of secretary, 29; referee, 57; garden, 65; sued for debt, 75; excuses accepted, 83; attack on by Stol, 104, 105; day and night school, 200
Van Kuyckendall, Jacob Luyersen, see Luyersen (Van Kuyckendall), Jacob
Van Linthout, Abraham, 279
Van Loosdrecht (Loserik), Jacob Hendricksen Maat, fighting, 111, 118, 254, 257; attachment of goods, 165, 168; complaint against, 169; summoned to court, 169; lot, 186; mentioned, 203, 271, 281;
   prosecuted by Dyckman, 116; for fighting, 254; by de Deckere, 261, 268, 270;
   sues Maria Jans, 187; Steven Jansen, 254, 259, 275;
   sued by Adriaensen, 153, 169; for payment for house, 254; by Jansen, 259; for debt, 268; by Pastoor, 272. *See also* Maat, Jacob Hendricksen
Van Naerden, Hendrick Jansen, *see* Jansen, Hendrick, the cowherd
Van Nes, Dirck, 29, **32**

Van Noortstrant, Jacob Janssen, 303
Van Putten (Van Petten), Wouter Aertsen, 20, 45
Van Rensselaer, Jan Baptista, court messenger sent to, 60; referee, 134; in possession of farm of Poest, 190; house nicknamed, 200; proposed actions against, 225; sued by Jan Hendricksen, 244; mentioned, 66, 158, 290
Van Schoonderwoert, **Teunis** Jacobsen, *see* Jacobsen, Teunis
Van Schoonderwoert, Rutger Jacobsen, *see* Jacobsen, Rutger
Van Slichtenhorst (Slechtenhorst), Brant Aertsen, assault on, 76, 83; announcement in church concerning, 99, 124; protest regarding, 119, 120; says court has no jurisdiction over him, 125; beavers due to Claes Gerritsen, 135, 142, 144; restitution of beavers, 228; mentioned, 15
Van Slingerlant, Teunis Cornelisen, 185, 268
Van Slyck, Cornelis, *see* Teunissen, Cornelis
Van Thienhooven, Cornelis, 62, 66
Van Twiller (Twillert), Jan (Johannes), 141, 186, 296
Van Valckenburgh, Herman Jansen, 203, 204, 206, 208
Van Valckenburgh, Lambert, summoned to court, 131; dispute with Herpertsen, 136; requests a lot, 185; testimony, 252;
   sued for debt, 34; by Goosen Gerritsen, 292
Van Vechten, Teunis Cornelisen, 233
Van Voorhout (Wip), Claes Cornelissen, 235
Van Voorhout, Seeger Cornelissen, *see* Cornelissen, Seeger
Van Westbroeck (Bos), Cornelis Teunissen, on committee to oversee surveying of lots, 16; appearance in court, 18;

Van Westbroeck (Bos), Cornelis
Teunissen — *Continued*
referee, 22, 44, 253; surety, 49,
263; letter to from members
of court, 113; memorandum
for, 114; magistrate, 126;
lease of house, 130; term of
office expired, 139; questioned
in court on various matters,
158, 168; loan of money to
Director General, 162; attorney, 275; requests lot for
Mingael, 297;
sues Jacobsen, 153; Croaet, 300
Van Ysselsteyn, Marten Cornelisen,
244
Vastrick, Gerrit, 137
Vastrick, Robbert, 137, 235
Vedder (Vetter), Harmen, 229
Veeder, Symon Volckertsen, *see*
Volckertsen, Symon
Verbeeck, Jan, takes burgher oath,
17; complaint about boy running
away, 22; referee, 27, 64, 254, 277;
to provide for support of church,
28; sued for debt, 29, 30; magistrate, 126, 236; sues Coninck, 149;
gives presents to Maquas, 171; on
committee to confer with Director
General, 174; appointed treasurer
of court, 214, 215; ordered to build
on lot, 263; mentioned, 164
Vervelen (Verwegen), Daniel, 225,
232
Visbeeck (Viesbeeck), Gerrit, 303
Visscher, Harmen Bastiaensen, *see*
Bastiaensen, Harmen
Vogel (Voogel), Arent Cornelisen,
35, 39, 40, 102, 207, 246
Volckertsen, Symon, baker, 67, 201
Vos, Cornelis, garden, 158; lot, 159;
loan of money to Director
General, 163; accused of giving nicknames to houses, 198;
house nicknamed, 201; missing
tub of butter, 209; summoned
to court for giving nicknames,
210; not guilty, 213; replication to answer filed by, 218;

Vos, Cornelis — *Continued*
sued by Adriaensen, 121; for
debt, 284; by Barentsen, 297,
301, 302, 305, 306
Vos, Hans, 248
Vosburgh, Abraham Pietersen, house,
15, 266; surveys by, 16, 17,
117; referee, 27; indebtedness,
102; petition to tap beer, 65;
part payment on bridges, 123;
to begin bridge, 138; faulty
surveying, 146; bridge not
built, 149; de Vos answers
complaints about, 155; lot,
158, 159, 213, 217, 245; petition
of, 160; ordered to appear in
court, 160–61, 164, 297; replication again to be sent to, 160,
164; arbitration of dispute,
173, wife, 174, 176; payment
for bridges, 178; sues Lammertsen, 235; disputed accounts, 281; mentioned, 112,
157;
sued for debt, 38, 58, 212, 235,
250; by Ryverdingh, 247; by
Pastoor, 247, 250, 253, 297,
301; by Maritge Dyckmans,
250; by Gerritsen, 274, 278; by
van Ekel, 291, 296, 298; by
Cobes, 297
Vrooman, Pieter Meussen, *see* Meussen (Messen), Pieter
Vylens, Claes, 302

Waeye, Keese, an Indian messenger,
156
Wemp, Jan Barentsen, 89, 209, 210.
See also Poest, Jan Barentsen
Wendel, Evert Jansen, 163, 199, 205,
226, 245
Wesselsen (Becker), Jochem, the
baker, wife, 17, 21, 26; pigsty,
22; judgment against, 48, 241;
to pay fine, 61–62, 66, 130, 249,
280; testimony in trial of
Jacob Stol, 103; attack on by
Stol, 105; to sheet bank of

Wesselsen (Becker), Jochem — Continued
    kill, 141; loan of money to Director General, 162; testimony regarding sale of brandy to savages, 164, 167; statement regarding nicknames of houses, 199; request concerning Jurriaensen's house, 199, 210, 238, 255; quarrel with Slichtenhorst, 227, 229, 234, 237, 241; petition presented by, 229; sells to savages, 242, 243; denies selling to savages, 250; gift for repairing Jurriaensen's house, 256; beavers in custody of, 274; request for a garden, 299;
    prosecuted for abusive language and assault, 23; for violating ordinance on baking, 55, 61, 251, 280; for fighting, 117, 130, 227, 229, 237, 238, 241; about beer found among savages, 213, 215; by de Deckere, 233, 248, 250, 277;
    sues Van Hoesen, 47, 49, 65; Rinckhout, 175; Hoffmeyer, 298;

Wesselsen (Becker), Jochem — Continued
    sued for slander, 18, 19, 25; for debt, 32; about a lot, 52, 119; by Labatie, 58; for assault, 73; for shooting a dog, 140; by Bamboes, 279; by Jacobsen, 282

Westerkamp, Femmetgen, 182. *See also* Alberts, Femmetgen

Westerkamp, Hendrick Jansen, wife, 26, 182; sued for debt, 32, 34; testimony, 62; mentioned, 73

Wever, *see* Martensen, Jan

Willems, Margriet, 22

Willemsen, Jacob, prosecuted for fighting, 117, 130; dispute about chest, 214, 215; petition presented by, 229; testimony, 241, 242; gift for repairing Jurriaensen's house, 256; sues Wesselsen, 274

Winnen (Winne), Pieter, 72. *See also* De Vlamingh, Pieter

Wip, Claes, *see* Van Voorhout, Claes Cornelissen

Witbeck, Jan Thomassen, *see* Thomassen, Jan

Witmont, Jan, 213, 214, 220

Witthardt (Withart), Jan, 134, 135

CANTO III

> THROUGH ME COME INTO THE CITY FULL OF PAIN
> THROUGH ME COME INTO ENDLESS SUFFERING
> THROUGH ME COME BE AMONG THE LOST
> I WAS FASHIONED BY MY HIGH MAKER IMPELLED
> BY JUSTICE; I WAS FASHIONED BY DIVINE POWER,
> BY UTTER WISDOM, BY ORIGINAL LOVE.
> BEFORE ME ONLY ETERNALS WERE CREATED
>   —ANGELS   HEAVEN   PRIMAL MATTER—
>   I GO ON FOREVER.
> YOU WHO COME IN ABANDON ALL HOPE.

Darkling these words I saw inscribed
atop a doorframe, so I said:

> "Master, the meanings are hard to me."

And like a man familiar with the site, he said:

> "Here all self-doubt must be cast off, and all cowardice
> snuffed out; we've come to the place I told you about
> where you'll see the sad beings bereft of the good
> of the intellect—the knowledge of God."

Then, face aglow, he put his hand on mine
—and I was comforted—and after that he led me in
to things concealed from the quick but not from the dead.
Here through the starless air sighs, cries and loud wails
reverberated; so first I wept. A motley clutch
of tongues, monstrous dialects, agony-words, spikes

CANTO III

> THROUGH ME COME INTO THE CITY FULL OF PAIN
> THROUGH ME COME INTO ENDLESS SUFFERING
> THROUGH ME COME BE AMONG THE LOST
> I WAS FASHIONED BY MY HIGH MAKER IMPELLED
> BY JUSTICE; I WAS FASHIONED BY DIVINE POWER,
> BY UTTER WISDOM, BY ORIGINAL LOVE.
> BEFORE ME ONLY ETERNALS WERE CREATED
> —ANGELS   HEAVEN   PRIMAL MATTER—
> I GO ON FOREVER.
> YOU WHO COME IN ABANDON ALL HOPE.

Darkling these words I saw inscribed
atop a doorframe, so I said:

> "Master, the meanings are hard to me."

And like a man familiar with the site, he said:

> "Here all self-doubt must be cast off, and all cowardice
> snuffed out; we've come to the place I told you about
> where you'll see the sad beings bereft of the good
> of the intellect—the knowledge of God."

Then, face aglow, he put his hand on mine
—and I was comforted—and after that he led me in
to things concealed from the quick but not from the dead.
Here through the starless air sighs, cries and loud wails
reverberated; so first I wept. A motley clutch
of tongues, monstrous dialects, agony-words, spikes

of wrath, faint and shrill voices and along with these
the thwack of hands—all created a tumult swirling
in a dun air outside of time, as sand eddies in a whirlwind.
And I, horror girding my head, said:

> "Master, what's this I hear, and who are these beings
> so in thrall to their grief?"

And he to me:

> "This despondency weighs down the miserable souls
> who in life earned neither praise nor blame, who here
> keep company with that craven choir of angels
> not rebels, not faithful to God, out for themselves only.
> Justly the heavens chased away such angels
> whom Hell's deeps rejected too, to make sure
> the infernal shades don't lord it over these cowards."

And I:

> "Master, what acute pain afflicts all the spirits here,
> who are breaking into lamentation?"

He answered:

> "I'll tell you, briefly. These, brought so low
> through the blindness of their lives, have no hope
> of death, and envy anyone else's fate.
> The world casts them out of its concerns.
> Pity scorns them; justice loathes them.
> Let's stop talking about them. Look and pass by."

I looked—and saw a banner whirling so fast
that I thought it could suffer no
pause; and behind it such a press of beings
that I would not have thought death
could undo so many.

As I was recognizing some,
I saw and knew the shade of him whose pettiness
of soul had spawned the Great Refusal. Immediately
certain, I understood that these were the malicious cabal
odious to God and to all His enemies. Green
flies and wasps stung these naked contemptible beings
—who'd never *been* alive—
and by their feet disgusting worms were harvesting
the mix of tears and blood that had streaked
their faces. And then peering further, I saw beings
on the bank of a wide river
so that I was moved to say:

> "Master, those beings I can just make out
> through the hazy light—can you tell me who they are,
> and what practice makes them seem so ready
> to cross over?"

And he to me:

> "You will understand these things when we pause
> on the sad banks of the Acheron."

Then, ashamed, eyes cast down because I was afraid
what I said had vexed him, I stopped talking
until we got to the river. Ah, an old man in a boat,
his hair turned white by time, was coming towards us,
shouting:

> "This is it, you depraved souls! Give up
> the hopes you'll see the sky again. I've come
> to bring you to the other shore forever dark—
> fire and ice. And you there, you living soul,
> quit the dead."

But when he saw I wasn't leaving, he said:

> "You may *not* go from here. You'll pass
> through another port of entry, in a different way;
> a lighter boat must carry you."

And my leader said to him:

> "Charon, don't torment yourself. This is how it must be,
> so ordered where will and power are one. Stand down."

And at once the scraggly jowls of the denatured
fen's boatman grew quiet; around his eyes fire
wheels were dancing. But as soon as the shades, naked
and worn, heard his menacing words, they grew
pallid and gnashed their teeth, blaspheming against God,
against their parents, against humankind, against the site,
the time, the seed that begot them, their birth.
Then they huddled together by that damned shore
which waits for every man who's not afraid
of God. Demon Charon of the ember eyes
beckons them, gathers them and drubs the laggards
with an oar.   As in the fall the leaves one after another
are subtracted from the branch, which sees those
spoils grounded, so at the infernal gesture Adam's bad
seed hurtle down from that shore, like falcons recalled.
That's how they go across the dark billows
and before they touch down on the other side, a new
band clusters on this shore.

The courteous master said:

> "My son, all beings who die in the wrath of God
> swarm here from every land, and they can't wait
> to cross the Acheron: divine justice so prods them
> that dread transforms into desire. No good soul
> ever comes by here, so if Charon calls you down
> you can now understand the drift of his words."

When he was done, the dusky surround shook
so strongly that I'm bathed in sweat as I remember
my fear. Through the tear-laden ground earth's
imprisoned winds touched off a scarlet flash
which downed my senses: and I fell like a man
snared by sleep.

CANTO IV

Thunder's intense crash ruptured my head's rapt
sleep; shocked like a man force wakes
I stood straight up and took my bearings;
my eyes refreshed I looked about—
what was this place? Ah, I found
myself on the cusp of the valley,
doleful chasm of infinite pain's roars, so dim
so profound, so hazy that I strained vainly,
could not glimpse a deep.

Face blanched the poet began:

> "Now let's go down *here,* into the blind
> world, me first you second."

And I, aware of his pallor, said:

> "How can I go if *you're* afraid, since it's you
> when I falter who are my comforter?"

And he said to me:

> "The anguish of the people down here daubs
> my face with that compassion you take for fear.
> Let's go, it's a long way that calls us."

So he went on and so had me go on too
into the first, abyss-girding, circle;
here, only through my ears' alert I grasped not
moan but sighs, which engendered
always quivering air, sighs of torqueless
grief in the huge crowds of babies, of women
and of men.

The benign teacher said to me:

> "These spirits you see, how is it you don't ask me
> who they are? Before you go any further
> I want you to know they haven't sinned
> but their merits do too little: no baptism, no door
> to the creed you accept. Born before Christianity,
> they loved God imperfectly.
>
> > I'm one of these beings.
>
> Such is the lack, not guilt, through which we're lost:
> shorn of hope we continue in desire."

When I heard him say this grief
clenched my heart: I knew precious beings
in this limbo, suspended. I wanted to be secure
in the fallacy-conquering faith, so I began:

> "Tell me teacher tell me gentle sir, did any being
> ever leave here through his own desert, or through
> another's, and later come to blessedness?"

He understood what I'd implied, answering:

> "I was new in this condition
> when I saw, arriving in this place,
> a being of power—crowned
> with victory's crossed halo—
>
> who drew from here the shade of our progenitor,
> of *his* son Abel, and the shade of Noah,
> of obedient Moses lawgiver,
> the shade of patriarch Abraham and king David,
> the shade of Jacob called Israel, with *his* father

16

> Isaac and *his* sons, and he drew out
> the shade of Rachel for whom Jacob did so much:
> he drew out many others
> —and lifted them to blessedness.
> And I want you to know that before these beings
> were saved no human souls were saved."

We went on as he talked, but still traversed
the forest, forest of thronged shades.
Near our way, the way of this side of sleep,
I saw fire had displaced a half-circle of dark;
and I a little far from it but near enough
could just about make out distinguished beings
holding that ground.

> "O you who honors science and art
> these beings whose merit sets them apart
> from the others' state—who are they?"

And he to me:

> "Their renown, resounding in the world above,
> earns grace from Heaven, and special place."

Right then I heard a voice:

> "Praise to the highest poet! The shade that went
> is back."

The voice stopped; silence; I saw
four great beings come near us, their faces
cast no sadness, no joy.

The benign teacher began:

> "Look at him, kingly, sword in hand, who leads
> the other three; that's Homer the supreme poet;

             next the satirist, Horace; then Ovid, and Lucan fourth.
             The single voice's utterance which honored me
             honors them too who share the high calling."

That's how I saw gathered together
the lovely school of that lord
of incandescent song: aquiline
he flies above them all. After talking
together for a time they turned to me
with signs of greeting, and my teacher
smiled on this. But there was more:
they made me one of them, I
sixth among that wisdom company.
So we went on as far as the semi-circle light
in conversation proper to the place
and which now to leave unreported
is beautiful.
             We came to the foot of a grand
castle within seven high concentric walls
surrounded by a sweet, protective stream
which—as if on firm land—we crossed;
with the wisdom company I penetrated
seven gates, arriving at fresh green grassland
that beings of great presence occupied.
What grave slow-moving eyes! How little
they spoke! And how soft their voices!
We moved from an edging of the green
into a high bright rise of open ground,
and could see those beings all in front of us
on the enameled meadow, major spirits
whose very being there exalted me.

I saw Electra with a multitude; I recognized
Hector, Aeneas and falcon-eyed Caesar-at-arms;
Across the field I saw Camilla the warrior
and Penthesilea the Amazon queen; I also saw

the Latian king, sitting with his daughter Lavinia,
Aeneas' wife; I saw that Brutus who brought down
the Tarquins—Lucretia, Julia daughter of Caesar,
Marcia wife of Cato, Cornelia. And I saw, sitting
alone, the sultan Saladin.

Then I raised my eyes a little bit and saw
Aristotle, *the master of those who know,*
seated among a family of philosophers; all
looked at him; all did him honor.
There I saw Socrates and Plato
in front of the others, and nearest to the master;
then Democritus, who called the world haphazard,
also Diogenes and Thales, Anaxagoras, Zeno,
Heraclitus and Empedocles. I saw the great
Dioscorides, collector of medicinal herbs;
I saw Orpheus, Cicero, Livy and Seneca
the moralist, the geometer Euclid, and Ptolemy,
Hippocrates, Galen, Avicenna and Averrhoes,
the maker of the Great Commentary.

How can I represent all these beings?
The tug of my theme so masters me
that my words often fail the facts.

Six becomes two: by a different way
my knowing teacher leads me
from silence to quaking air,
and I come to a lightless place.

CANTO V

So I went from the first circle down
to the second, which girds a smaller space.
So much more pain—a goad to keening.
Ghastly Minos, snarling inquisitor of sinners
decides at the entrance and consigns
as his tail curling rings his body; I mean
the number of tailcoils marks
a Hell-rank for each accused ill-born soul
coming and confessing. Before the judge
the crowds appear, perpetual, every soul
by turn speaking, hearing, hurled
under.

When Minos saw me, he left his extensive
operation, and he said to me:

> "You who come to this sad site, watch out:
> beware of how you enter and whom you trust
> and don't be fooled by the vast way in."

And my guide said to him:

> "Why persist? Why cry havoc? Don't block
> the way his fate assigns: the way is willed
> where will is power. No more meddling."

Now I begin to hear the music
of suffering; now I've come
where massive baying beats at me.

I came to a place, mute of light,
roaring like a tempest-stricken sea

beset by roiling winds. Pillaging, the hellish
gale without a pause in its ferment
sucks the spirits in, smites them,
whirls them around—molestation. The spirits
arrive in front of the ruin: shrill cries,
grief, lamentation, and the spirits
blaspheming against divine power.
I learned such scourging damns fleshly
sinners whose reason's in thrall to appetite.
As starlings in a sweeping crowd
are conveyed by their wings in the cold
so are the wicked spirits driven here
and there by the racking suspiration
of the air, driven down, driven up.
Peace is denied them—even hope for less pain.

As cranes chant laments while they course
in a long line in air, so—as I saw—did the gale-
driven shades approach, wailing.

So I said:

        "Master, who are these beings so flayed
        by the black air?"

Then he said to me:

        "One foremost among those you ask about,
        an empress, ruled over speakers of far-flung
        tongues; she was rotted by the itch of lust,
        so much so that she made her law
        sanction that vice to mask her violations.
        She's Semiramis the wife of Ninus, who succeeded
        him and held the land the Sultan rules.
        Next is the woman who for love took her life
        and betrayed Sychaeus' ashes; then

> wild Cleopatra. Look: Helen, center
> of evil whirling years; and see: great Achilles
> who driven by love ended in battle.
> See Paris, Tristan . . ."

And he showed me many more shades
and named them as he pointed, shades
ripped from life by love. I heard my teacher
name the ladies and the knights and pity
seized me, my bearings nearly lost.

I began:

> "Poet, I'd like to speak to those two beings
> passing by together, wind-lifted, who seem
> so light."

And he to me:

> "You'll see when they come nearer to us, then
> make your appeal; say: 'By Love your governor'
> and they will come."

Wind-enfolded, they were borne to us
and right away I called to them, saying:

> "O worn spirits come talk with us
> if Another allows."

As doves, summoned by desire, are moved
by their will through the air on still, extended
wings and arrive at the sweet nest,
so did these two shades leave the consort
where Dido is, coming to us
through the baneful air, so strong
my affectionate outcry.

> "O gracious, gentle alive being who travel
> through the purple-black air on your visit
> to us who have dyed the world incarnadine,
> if the universe's king were our friend
> we'd beseech him to grant you peace
> because you're moved to pity by our perversity.
> While the wind here stills we'll listen to you
> and we'll talk with you: whatever pleases you
> to hear and to say.
>   I was born in a city
> by the shore of the sea to which the river Po
> fronting its heeling streams goes down to find peace.
> Love, which quickly fires the gentle heart,
> struck my lover with need for my beauty—
> from which I was remorselessly subtracted—
> and I'm wounded, still, by how it happened.
>
> Love constrains the beloved to love the lover
> and you can see he so delighted me
> that love has not abandoned me.
> Love steered us to one death.
> In lowest Hell Caina waits for the man
> who turned off our lives."

When I listened to these wretched souls
I bowed my head and held it down so long
that finally the poet said to me:

> "What are you thinking?"

When I could answer, I started:

> "O just think how many sweet thoughts,
> how much desire have led these beings
> to the way of woe."

Then I turned towards them and I
started again:

> "Francesca, out of sadness and pity I am weeping
> for your agony. But tell me, in your gentle
> soughing intervals together, how and in what way
> did love acquaint you with your dubious desires?"

And she to me:

> "A happy day recalled in a time of pain outweighs
> all other suffering. Your teacher knows this.
> But if you want so much to know our love's
> very root, I'll tell you weeping in telling. One day
> we read for pleasure of Lancelot and the tug of love:
> we were alone all unawares. Often as we read
> our eyes would meet and our faces grow pale
> but one point only pulled us down.
> When we read of the longed-for smiling lips
> kissed by a lover like that,
> the one who'll never be severed from me, trembling,
> kissed my mouth. That book was our go-between
> and so the writer too. We read no more that day."

As one spirit was saying this
the other moaned, and I afflicted
by pity fainted as if I'd died,
dropping like a corpse.

CANTO VI

Closed down before the pathos of the yoked lovers
whose agony has so exquisitely disordered me
my mind comes back and all about me
as I move, as I turn, as I watch
I see new tortures and the newly tortured.

I'm in the third circle—rain without end:
abominable, cold and fierce, no tack
no shift in its rhythm or condition.
Through the murky air huge hailstones, foul
water and snow spill onto the receiving ground
and Cerberus, triple-throated beast, vicious,
bizarre, is baying like a hound
over the sodden tribe in the stinking fill.
His eyes the vividest red, his oily beard black,
his hands clawed and his belly jutting
he scrapes the spirits and he skins them
and he quarters them. Rain-smitten, doglike
they howl; for refuge they often muddle
from one flank to the next, the sacrilegious
wretches, rotating.   When Cerberus, huge worm,
beheld us, all limbs astir he opened his mouths
and displayed his fangs. With hands spread my guide
gathered in some dirt and flung fistfuls
into the avid maws. As a craving dog barks
and calms down, embattled then engrossed
when it bites down on its feed, that's what happened
with the three disgusting snouts of demon Cerberus—
whose routine hollers make souls yearn
for a shutdown in their hearing. We slogged over the shades
brought down by the pelting rains, stepping

through the emptiness of these lifelike wraiths.
They lay on the ground, all of them, except for one
who sat up as soon as he perceived us passing by.

He said to me:

          "O you, led through this Hell, you were made
          before I was undone; if you can,
          remember me."

And I to him:

          "Maybe the wrack of your anguish hauls you
          out of my mind, so it does seem to me
          I've never seen you; but tell me: who are you,
          set down in this sorrow-place and prone
          to such correction—some might be worse,
          none so sickening."

And he to me:

          "Your city like a sac brims over with the slops
          of its suffusing envy. How it held me in cloudless
          times! You citizens, you called me Ciacco the Hog.
          Through the damned sin of gluttony
          I'm exhausted under the rain, as you see,
          and not alone in my pain: all these shades
          are suffering the same way for the same fault."

That's all he said. I answered:

          "Ciacco, I'm on the verge of tears as I feel your
          anguish weigh on me. But tell me, if you know,
          the fate of citizens in the divided city, say
          if any there are just, and tell me too
          the cause of all that strife."

And he to me:

        "After long discord, blood; and the faction
        from outside seizing the offensive will drive
        the other out. Within three of the sun's courses
        in the wake of a cabal the first group,
        tearful and angry, will fall and the other
        long holding its head high will rise
        through cunning designs by one who now's
        equivocal. The city holds two just men,
        ignored; the city's hearts have burst
        into flame; three sparks have kindled them:
        pride, envy and avarice."

Here he stopped his rending words, and I to him:

        "Teach me again with the gift of your voice.
        Farinata and Tegghiaio, such worthy men,
        Iacopo Rusticucci, Arrigo and Mosca—
        who meant well. Tell me where they are, tell
        about them: I'm seized by a great wish to know
        if they're soothed by Heaven or soured by Hell."

And he:

        "They're among the blackest souls:
        they're weighed down deep by various faults;
        If you arrive at that level you can see them
        but when you'll be in the sweet world
        please bring me back to memory.
        I won't say more, nor answer again."

He averted his eyes, which had so directly
engaged mine, went crosseyed,
looked at me briefly, dropped his head

and fell again among the blind.
And my guide said to me:

          "He won't wake up again until the angel trumpet
          sounds and the exacting judge arrives. Each
          will see his sad tomb again, take on flesh and form
          and hear what booms throughout eternity."

So, slowly, we passed through the filthy
mixture of shade and rain, touching a little
on the life to come, and so I said:

          "Teacher, these torments—will they grow worse
          after the great judgment or decrease
          or stay the same?"

And he to me:

          "Refer to your science, to Aristotle: the more
          perfect the being the greater the pleasure,
          and the pain. These damned, who will never attain
          true perfection, will be nearer then than now."

We went around that curving road,
saying more than I set down
and we came to the point where the way down
starts. Here we found Plutus the great enemy.

CANTO VII

Cackling Plutus started:

> "Pape Satan, Pape Satan, aleppe!"

To calm me down the kind all-knowing sage said:

> "Don't be afraid: no matter how strong he is
> he can't block our way down this rock."

Then he veered and fixing that bloated face said:

> "Hold off hell-wolf, you're fodder for your own
> rage; this descent has its reasons in the will
> of Heaven, where archangel Michael avenged
> the adulterous uprising."

As wind-bellied sails crumple when the mast gives
way, that's how the fierce beast buckled.
Then we went below into the fourth depression
and deeper yet into the sad hemming-in tilt
bounding the engorging evil of all the world.
Ah, justice of God who here compress such gluts
of the new griefs and pains that I've seen!
And why do our sins so waste us? Like the waves there
in the whirlpool Charybdis which, meeting, crash,
these souls in surge and reflux dance their dances as they have to.

Here on both sides I saw more people
than at any other site; uttering great wails
they strained their chests against huge
rocks and slammed into each other as they met.
Then every spirit turned, rolling his stone

anew, and yelled Why hoard? and Why waste?
Jeering they all came back around the dismal circle
to the point across from where they'd been
and joined the other joust.
        And I,
I felt as if my heart had been pierced through
and I said:

        "Show me now my teacher who the people are;
         these tonsured ones on our left—all clergy?"

And he to me:

        "All. In the first life their squinty minds'-eyes
        were heedless of right measure. All—tightly mean
        or disbursing rank gifts. You can tell by what
        they snarl; riven by their antithetical faults
        they pull in to those two opposing points of the circle.
        These spirits with the shorn heads, men of the
        cloth, both popes and cardinals, were slaves to avarice."

And I:

        "Teacher, among these shades I'm sure I could place
        a few at least who've been stained
        with such uncleanliness."

And he to me:

        "A vain hope; because their blind lives fouled them
        they're now opaque to anyone's apprehension.
        In the thrall of clashes, time everlasting,
        these will rise from death fist shut and *those*
        the shorn be prodigal to the very hair. The rank
        gifting and the niggard fist have cost them
        Heaven the lovely otherworld and set them

                brawling. That's how it is, no pretty words.
                Now my son you can see, entrusted to Fortune,
                the brief comedy of goods in which humankind
                traffics; because all the gold that ever was or is
                under the moon could give no rest
                to a single worn-out soul."

I said to him:

                "Teacher, tell me more: this Fortune you mentioned
                to me—who is she whose claws so wrap
                around the riches of the world?"

And he to me:

                "O so foolish, so bedeviled by ignorance; here,
                feed on this, my sense of who she is. He
                whose wisdom transcends everything made
                the heavens and gave them guides, each measuring
                out from part to part the same bodies of light,
                shining. In the same way for the grand world
                he ordained a general minister and guide who in ripe
                time and outside human sway would shift barren
                keepings from country to country, from one being
                to another: her decree, hidden like a serpent
                in grass, selects the rulers *and* the pining. No
                knowledge of yours has the power to withstand her.

                Like the other powers of Heaven she can see
                what's to be; she comes to judgments; she
                keeps up her kingdom. She is change, driven
                swift by necessity, so often do so many wait
                their turn. They target *her,* those very men
                who curse and should be praising her—who's taxed
                with guilt by their rumors and so berated
                undeservedly.

                                But she, blessed, will hear
                    none of this; she's happy with the other primal
                    beings and turns her sphere in the light of bliss.

                    Now let's go down to greater pain. The stars
                    that were rising when I started out are sinking now
                    and staying longer is forbidden."

We crossed the circle to the other bank
passing by a spring that boils up and rushes out
into a linked gully, the water purplish-black,
and we moving along by its drab waves went
down an odd path. Into the bog Styx this sad rivulet
arrives, after coursing to the foot of the grey
malign slopes. And I at a standstill stared fixedly
at naked people steeped in bog-mud, and wrathful.
They slammed each other not only with their hands
but also with their heads and chests and feet
and rent one another with their teeth.
My good teacher said:

                    "My son, here you see souls overcome by rage
                    and I must tell you too that under the water
                    people are sighing, producing the surface bubbles
                    your roaming eyes see. Set in slime they say:
                      'In the sweet air the sun makes happy
                      we were sullen; we harbor now within us
                      a sluggish fog and now we brood
                      in the black ooze.'
                    Because their speech is marred they foam
                    this hymn in a throaty gurgle."

And so we went, describing a great arc
at the dirty pond which lay between the dry
bank and the slop, our eyes turned to those
swilling muck, and we came at last to a tower's foot.

CANTO VIII

Picking up my story, I have this to tell:
long before we arrived at the foot of the high
tower, our eyes, drawn by two pitchlights
set at the peak, traveled upward; another
flare, so far off it was hard to see, blazed back.
And I turned to the All-Wisdom Ocean and said:

"What does this mean? and what's
the other fire's answer? and
who set the signal?"

And he to me:

"Over the stinking waves you can already
glimpse what's coming, unless
the marsh-haze hides it."

No arrow sprung from its bowcord ever pierced
air more nimbly than the bantam boat which hove
into view right then, its single steersman yelling:

"Now you've had it, galled soul."

My master said:

"Phlegyas, Phlegyas—you're shouting into
a void; we're yours only for the time it takes
to negotiate the fen."

Phlegyas, in his tamped fury, was like
a being who in building vexation hears
he's been taken by a massive swindle.

My guide stepped into the boat and had me
follow and only when I entered did it dip.
As soon as he and I had ventured
down, the worn prow, sawing ahead, rode
deeper than it would have with any others.
As we cut across the clotted channel
a mud-enfolded figure manifested
before me and said:

        "Your hour hasn't come. Who are you?"

And I to him:

        "If I come I don't stay. But you, so hideous,
         who are you, what happened?"

He answered:

        "As you see—I'm one who cries."

And I to him:

        "You, damned, stay where you belong, stuck
         in your grief and your wailing—
         through your shrouding
         muck I know you."

Both his hands reached for the boat; alert,
my master drove him back, saying:

        "Get back, with all the other dogs!"

After that, throwing his arms around my neck,
kissing my face, my master said:

"How seemly, soul, your indignation; blessed
the woman who gave you birth! In the world
this man's pride puffed him up and no good
attends his memory. That's why his shade's
enraged. So many beings up above who act
now like kingly beings will bed
down in this bog like pigs
—having left behind
a terrible scorn."

And I:

"Master, before we leave the lake I'd love
to see him pitched into this broth."

And he to me:

"Be content; you will, before you catch
a glimpse of the landing; a wish like yours
will be granted."

And soon I saw the mudbeings so torment him
that I stlll give praise and thanks to God for it.
They were all yelling: 'Get Filippo Argenti!'
and the seething Florentine shade turned on himself
with his teeth. There we left him; I have nothing
more to tell. But a keening broke violently
upon my ears and then, my sight wiped clean,
I peer ahead, rapt. The good master said:

"Now my son: the city of Dis nears, with its
sober subjects, its grand battalions."

And I:

> "Master, there, in the valley, I clearly see
> its mosques—vermillion, as if charged by fire."

And he said to me:

> "Made other by the city's endless fire,
> they're aglow, as you see, with a suffusing
> redness in this lower Hell."

Pushing on, we reached the deep ditches girding
the disconsolate city, whose walls seemed to me
to be made of iron. Only after a number of passes
did the steersman shout:

> "Out. Here's the entrance."

I saw—atop the gates—more than a thousand rebel
angels who once had rained from Heaven, and who
furious, yelled:

> "What being is this, without death, who moves
> through the kingdom of the dead?"

And my teacher, All-Wisdom Ocean, gestured
his wish for a secret talk with them. Then
somewhat stifling their vast disdain, they said:

> "Come alone; this being who's braved the kingdom
> must go back on his own lunatic path and test
> his way; you, his guide in the obscure, you
> will stay."

Reader, consider my heartache at the baleful
charge: I believed I'd never get back to the living
world. I said:

> "O my sweet leader, many times, seven times
> and more, you've renewed me and you've
> plucked me from a menacing dread.
>
> Don't leave me so disordered,
>
> and if we're to be denied
> let's go back together."

And my lord, who'd brought me there,
said to me:

> "Don't be afraid; no one can impede our journey.
> It is given. But wait for me here; comfort
> your weary spirit and feed it with hope. I will not
> abandon you in this lower Hell."

He goes; and there the tenderhearted father
leaves me in doubt, awash in no and yes.
I couldn't hear what he proposed, but after
the brief parley, they all scattered in a stumbling
rush and they—our enemies—they slammed the gates
in the face of my lord, left outside, and he turned
back to me, steps thick.
                    Eyes cast down, all daring
lopped from his brow, he said between sighs:

> *"They* would keep me out of the sad world?"

And to me he said:

> "Don't let my anger upset you: I will overcome them
> no matter what defensive plans they hatch inside.
> Theirs is an old arrogance, once flaunted at a gate
> that's a pass-through now, still unbarred. You saw it,
> under its fateful writing. And within it, one is

already coming down the slope, crossing the circles alone. Through him—for us— the city will be penetrated."

CANTO IX

My guide was turning back; seeing my craven face
grow wan as I saw him spurned, he swiftly
checked the tinted rise of his quickened
annoyance. On the alert, he stopped—like a man
who listens—his eye unable to travel on
through the murky air and through the rank
fog. He began:

> "Still, it's fitting we should win this fight;
> if not. . . . There *was* an offer; we wait in hope
> for that expected being; it's taking so long!"

When he veiled his start with the words
that trailed it, those words—it was clear to me—
did differ from the ones that came before, but
they scared me anyway: I may have drawn
from that cleft utterance an import sharper
than he'd intended. I asked:

> "The only punishment in Limbo is the end
> of hope: does anyone from there ever come
> down this deep, to this sad declivity?"

And he answered me:

> "It's rare that any of us follow this path I'm on.
> It *is* true I was down here once before, compelled
> by that terrible conjure woman Erichto,
> who used to call incorporeal spirits
> back to their bodies.
>
>   I had not long lost my flesh
> before she made me go inside those walls,

39

>   to the Judas Circle, to tear a shade away from there.
>   It's the deepest darkest place, the furthest away
>   from all-encircling Heaven. I know the way well;
>   be comforted. This bog, with its stinking exhalations,
>   belts the sad city—which strife alone will open to us."

And he said more, but I can't remember it
because my eyes had drawn me utterly
to the glowing top of the high tower which held
—already risen—three infernal bloodflecked
Furies endowed with women's arms and legs
and bearing and arrayed with shining green
hydras and for hair small snakes and horned
serpents winding round the feral temples.
And he, well acqainted with the bondwomen
of the Queen of Endless Grieving, said to me:

>   "Look at the violent Furies. That's Megara
>   on the left; the one on the right, howling,
>   Alecto; between them is Tesiphone."

He was quiet.
            They tore at their own breasts
with their nails, they scourged themselves
with their palms, their cries so wild I clutched
at the poet out of fear. Looking down they said:

>   "Let's get Medusa here and we'll turn him into stone.
>   We tried, and failed, to avenge Theseus' assault."

>   "Turn and keep your eyes shut; if the Gorgon
>   shows herself and you see her, you'll never
>   get back above."

That's what my master said, and he himself
turning me around, distrustful of the work
of my hands, put his own on my eyes also.

O you whose understanding is whole,
note the teaching hidden under the veil
of these strange lines.
                      And now over the roiled
waves a terrifying sound—which caused both
shores to tremble—burst, a wildness of hot
winds contending, like a turbulence that strikes
a forest and unrestrainedly cracks twigs
and hurls them beyond the woods as the dust
before it and beasts and shepherds fly.
He freed my eyes and said:

> "Now direct the vitals of your eyes over
> that age-old scum to where the mist sours."

As frogs before their enemy the snake
scatter throughout the water, each
ending up in a squat on the bottom, so I saw
more than a thousand wracked souls
break before one who was crossing the Styx
on foot, soles dry. He cleared away
that fetid air from his face, often
moving his left hand in front of him;
it was only *that* travail that made him appear
weary. He must have been sent from Heaven.
I turned to the master, whose gesture indicated:
Be quiet. Bow to the messenger—who seemed
to me disdainful, arriving unopposed at the gate
which he opened with a small wand.
On the dread threshold he began:

> "You, outcasts of Heaven, contemptible body,
> this insolence within you—where's it from?
> Why do you balk at that will whose intent
> can never be thwarted, which has increased

> your pain a number of times? Why butt
> against the fates? Your Cerberus, if you recall,
> still pays the price, his chin and neck
> excoriated."

Then he turned, going back by the scummy path
and didn't say a word to us, but looked
like a man beset and stung by other cares
than those of the beings in front of him.
And feeling safe after the holy words
we stepped out toward the city, we entered
there without constraint and I, eager
to look over the state of such a citadel,
peered intently all around as soon as I was in
and saw on every hand a great expanse
filled with pain and vicious torments.
Just as at Arles, where the Rhone becomes
stagnant, and at Pola near Quarnero—which
encloses Italy and bathes her borders—
sepulchers dot the parceled ground, so they did
in every segment here, but how much more
bitter *these* tombs, aglow all over from the ground's
scattered flames and hot beyond the need of any smith's
craft. Their lids were up and such deeply pained
wails rose up from them as could only come
from the sad and from the suffering.
And I said:

> "Master, who are these beings, buried inside
> those tombs, so present in their aching sighs?"

And he to me:

> "Here are the foremost heretics and their cohorts
> of every sect, and the graves are loaded down
> more heavily than you're imagining; like lies

with like and the tombs are heated more and heated less."

Then he turned to the right, and we passed between the afflictions and the battlements.

CANTO X

Keeping to a secluded lane between
those afflictions and the city walls,
my master now goes on, with me close
behind. I started:

> "O perfection of reason: you at your pleasure
> steering me through the iniquitous circles—
> talk to me, feed my yearning. The beings
> lying inside the burial vaults—can they be seen?
> The lids are raised already and no one's
> keeping guard."

And he to me:

> "They'll all be encased when they come back here
> from Jehoshaphat with the bodies they left up
> above. This cemetery parcel holds Epicurus and all
> his followers, who believe that the soul dies
> with the body. About your question: you'll find
> an answer to it here, as well as a response
> to the longing you've been hiding from me."

And I:

> "Good guide, I shroud my heart from you
> only to husband my speech—you've been
> instilling *that* in me."

> "O Tuscan crossing alive over the fiery city,
> so deferential in your words, would you linger
> in this place, please? Your dialect reveals
> your origin in that august homeland which—
> maybe—I afflicted in my overzealous rigor."

These words issued suddenly from one
of the vaults so, frightened, I edged slightly
nearer to my guide and he said to me:

      "Turn around. What's wrong? Look there—
      you can see that Farinata's raised himself;
      you can gauge his height from the waist up."

I had my eyes already fixed on his; his chest
and forehead were lifting as if to show his vast
contempt for Hell. And my guide's bold, quick
hands pushed me between the vaults towards
Farinata, saying:

      "Find the right words."

When I got to the foot of Farinata's tomb,
he glanced at me and then—scornfully I'd say—
asked me:

      "Who were your people?"

Eager to obey, I hid nothing but told all,
at which he superciliously said:

      "They were such brutal enemies to me, to mine
      and to my party that I scattered them twice."

I answered him:

      "Yes, you expelled them, though both the first
      and second times all came back from each
      banishment—but your people never did master
      the art of return."

Then alongside him a vaulted shade exposed
to the chin came into view; I think he'd got onto
his knees; then after scrutinizing all the space
around me (as if he hoped to find another being
in my company), plaintively—all expectation spent—
he said:

                    "If your extraordinary skill allows you passage
                      through this blind keep, where's my son
                      and why isn't he with you?"

And I to him:

                    "I don't come here through my own power.
                    The one who's waiting over there is leading me
                    through this place; perhaps your son Guido
                    despised him."

Having already construed his words
and the make-up of his painful sanctions,
I knew his name and I could answer
unstintingly. Suddenly up, he cried:

                    "What do you mean, 'despised'? Isn't he still alive?
                    Sweet light no longer sails onto his eyes?"

When he became aware that I was putting off
my answer, he fell face up, and after that—
incommunicado.   But I'd been stayed
by great-hearted Farinata's 'linger in this place,
please.' His face now stolid, head unmoving,
body set, he took up where he'd left off:

                    "If they've studied the returner's art poorly,
                    that torments me more than this bed.
                    The face of lunar Hecate, who reigns here,

>   will be rekindled just under fifty times
>   before you understand that art's charge.
>   As you hope ever to return to the sweet world,
>   tell me: why are the Florentines in their laws
>   so cruel to my people?"

I said to him:

>   "The chaos and the butchery that crimsoned
>   the river Arbia: these explain Florence's actions."

Then he sighed and shook his head and said:

>   "I wasn't alone in that, but only a good reason
>   would have prompted me to join my fellow
>   Ghibbelines in battle. Where everyone agreed
>   that Florence should be flattened, I, only I, was
>   the one man before them all to plead for her."

I beseeched him:

>   "So that your seed find rest some time, unravel
>   this knot which has my mind in thrall: if
>   what I hear is right, it seems that you in Hell
>   can foresee what Time will bear in its wake,
>   but the present is closed to you."

He said:

>   "Our sight is troubled in this place. The Great
>   Presence allots to us, still, a certain
>   shining, through which we're able to see
>   what's far away; our minds give out
>   when things come near or here; unless
>   messengers arrive to bring us word,
>   we know nothing of your human state.

> So you can understand that at the final closing
> of the future's door, everything we know
> will die."

I felt such qualms about my earlier silence
that I said:

> "Would you tell the fallen being
> his son is still one with the living.
> And if I was mute in my response
> just now, let him know that my attention
> was already harboring the mistake
> that you've just corrected."

At that my master called me back
and so, more hurriedly, I implored
the spirit to tell me who were there
with him. He said to me:

> "I'm lying here with more than a thousand.
> Frederic the Second is inside, and Ottaviano
> the Cardinal. I'm not saying a thing
> about the others."

With that he hid himself, and I stepped
toward the age-old poet, thinking over
Farinata's utterance, which I considered
hostile. My guide set out and then,
as we picked our way forward
he said to me:

> "Why is your mind crossed?"

I satisfied him wholly,
and the sage said to me:

> "Fix in your mind whatever you've heard said
> against you. And now, here, pay attention."

He pointed, forcefully.

> "When you face the sweet radiance of the being
> whose beautiful eyes encompass everything—
> from her you'll know the journey of your life."

He turned left: aiming for the middle
we quit the wall and took a path dropping
to a valley whose rising stink
—however high we were—
disgusted us.

CANTO XV

Right now one of the harsh banks conveys us
and up above, the rivermist hovers,
and screens water and embailkinents from the fire.
As the Flemings, from Wissant to Bruges,
afraid of the impinging flood
set up their dikes to blunt the sea-threat
and as the Paduans of Carentana, along the Brent's edges,
shore up their castles and towns
against the snowmelt torrents
so did *these* mounds, of like construction,
rise, though their architect, whoever he was,
had made them neither as high, nor as wide.
We walked so far beyond the wood
that even if I'd turned to the rear
I couldn't have made it out.
Then we came upon a company of souls
walking by the bank; and everyone
peered at us as men under a new moon
will gaze each at each;
squinting, they peered at us,
like an old tailor into his needle's eye.
As we were being eyed by the tribe of shades
I was recognized by one of them, who seized the hem
of my gown and cried out,

"Amazing. Is it *you?*"

And I, when he stretched out his arm to me,
peered so intently at his baked face
that even his scorched features
couldn't prevent my recognizing *him*
and lowering my face to his face

I answered:

        "Ser Brunetto. It's *you*! here?"

And he:

        "O my son, please don't be annoyed
        if Brunetto Latini turns back to walk with you
        a little, and lets the others go their way."

I said to him:

        "Yes, with a full heart
        as much as I'm able;
        if you want me to sit with you,
        I'll do it, if my guide will let me."

He said:

        "My son, if any being in this flock
        stop walking for even a second, the fire will eat
        at him for a hundred years.
        So move on; I will follow you closely
        And soon will rejoin my company,
        which goes on mourning endless loss."

I didn't dare to step down to his level
but kept my head inclined
as in a reverential stance.
He said to me:

        "What fortune or what fate
        has brought you here before your time,
        and who's your guide on this path?"

I answered him:

"In earth's tranquil life
before I attained
to a fullness of years
I wandered in a valley,
but just yesterday I turned my back on it.
This man appeared when I was losing ground again,
and by this path now leads me home."

And he:

"As long as you're guided by your star,
you will not fail to reach fair harbor;
if I'd judged you well in our life on earth
if I hadn't died so early in my life—
seeing that Heaven makes its face to shine upon you—
I would have cheered you on in your work,
but those malign, ungrateful people
with rockhard mountain hearts
who came down from old Fiesole
will fall on you for your good works.
That's how things should be: it isn't right
that the sweet fig should come to fruit
among the sour serviceberries.
Common knowledge asserts those men are blind,
envious, arrogant, greedy.
Rid yourself of their usages; be sure to do it.
Your future is signed with such honor
that the factions will both hunger after you,
but the grass will forever elude those goats.
Let the beasts of Fiesole eat
themselves: on their dunghill some plants may bear
the sacred seed of brave Romans
who stayed and did not move to Florence;
such plants are never for the beasts of Fiesole,
denizens of wickedness and vice."

I answered him:

>"If I had my wish,
>you would not have lost your human place:
>you live in my mind, how clearly
>I remember you, sweet and fatherly,
>when, for hour and hour on end in the world,
>you used to teach how man makes himself eternal.
>What I owe you my tongue will declare all my life.
>What you tell me of my coming fate
>I will note down, and save with other texts
>to submit to one who knows, if I can arrive at that Lady.
>There's a thing I need to say to you:
>with a clean conscience
>I am prepared for Fortune; whatever happens.
>I'm not new to such prophecy;
>let Fortune spin her wheel
>and the churl strike with his mattock."

My guide now turned around, to his right,
And looked at me and said:

>"A good listener hears."

Without responding, I walked ahead
And talked with Ser Brunetto, asking
about his fellow shades, which best-born
and which most famous.
And he to me:

>"Some deserve words; others silence.
>There wouldn't be enough time for such talk.
>In brief, we were men of worth, clerics, all of us—
>Scholars of great renown, who on the earth
>Were all polluted with the same sin.
>There's Priscian the grammarian, with that sad bunch,

     And with him is Francesco of Accorso, the Oxford law
                   professor.
     If you had any wish to see such scum
     look at that man there, who stiff in his iniquity
     was moved from Arno to the Bacchiglione by the Pope
     —the Servants' Servant!—and died unnatural.
     I'd say more, but here's an end to talk;
     I see a new dustcloud rising from the sand,
     and new people approach, not *my* shades.
     To your care I commend my Treasure.
     My name lives on in it; I ask no more."

Then he turned back and ran, like one of those
who across the plain at Verona race for the green cloth;
and as he ran, he seemed
the one who wins, not the one who loses.

CANTO XXI

So, crossing from bridge to bridge,
we were talking about matters
that my Comedy doesn't care
to sing. We reached the bridge's
crest and stopped there to contemplate
the next worthless sobs and the further pit
of Malebolge, which I saw eerily dark.
As artisans at the Venice Arsenal boil
gluey pitch in wintertime to stop up
their run-down dry-docked ships—
one worker building his craft anew,
another caulking his travel-weary vessel's
ribs, this artisan hammering away
at the prow, that one at the stem,
others making oars, some twining strands
of hemp, a worker patching a jib
and a mainsail—
                    so not by dint of fire but through
God's art a sticky viscid pitch down there clung
to the banks on every side. I saw the pitch
but in it only the driven bubbles that the boil
raised, the whole swelling and collapsing, swelling
and collapsing. While I was transfixed
by what I was viewing, my guide, saying:

                    "Look out, look out!"

drew me to him from my spot on the bridge's
edge. Then I turned
                    like a man undone
by sudden terror who longs to see
what he's running from,

                          like a man who keeps
looking as he bolts; and I saw behind us a black
devil approach, running up the craggy ridge.
His look struck me as really ferocious, how
dire he seemed to me in his doings—
the lightness of his feet, the fanned-out wings!
On his proud peaked shoulder lay both
thighs of a sinner, whose pedal tendons
his claws clutched. From our bridge, he said:

> "Hey Vileclaw here's one of the Saint Zita
> elders: shove him under; I'm going back
> to that well-stocked town for more of them,
> all public swindlers, except for Bonturo
> —sure. Money there makes No mean Yes."

He tossed the sinner down, then veered
to the hard bluff: no mastiff off the leash
ever rushed faster to catch a thief.
The sinner plummeted; he came back up
pitch-blackened ass first, but the demons
under the bridge's cover yelled:

> "There's no *Sacred Visage* image here; here
> you don't swim as you do in the Sperchio
> River; so unless you're up for our gaffs
> don't jut out beyond the pitch."

Then they bit at him with more than a hundred
grappling hooks and said:

> "Here's where you have to dance, under cover,
> to carry on your dirty tricks—if you can."

It's in this way that cooks have their scullions
plunge pot-forks right into the middle of kettles

to keep the meat from floating up. The good master
said to me:

> "Protect yourself: squat behind a craggy rock
> so that none of the demons can see you
> and don't be afraid of any affront to me:
> I've got things under control here and had to deal
> with a set-to like this one once before."

At that he moved beyond the bridgehead
and as he reached the sinkhole that was pit six
he had to show himself unruffled. With the fury
and the agitation of a dog swarm plaguing
a down-and-outer who stops on a dime and begs
right there, the demons rushed against my guide
from under the bridge, their hooks at the ready.
But he called out:

> "Let your malice go! Before you take me
> with your hooks one of you come up and
> hear what I have to say; then get together—
> decide if I'm to be gaffed."

All of them shouted:

> "Viletail!"

One of them moved (the others keeping their places)
and came forward wondering:

> "What good will it do him?"

My master said:

> "You think, Viletail, that you see me here—
> prepared and firm in face of all your defenses—

> without God's will and fateful intervention?
> Let us through: it's willed in Heaven
> that I show another being this wild way."

Then, the pride of Viletail fallen, the hook
dropping to his feet, he said to his band:

> "In that case, we can't touch him."

And my guide said to me:

> "You, crouched among the bridge's rocks,
>   it's safe for you now to come back to me."

So I moved and quickly came to him, the devils
in such a press I was afraid they would renege.
That was how, once, I saw some soldiers—under
treaty—leaving the Castle at Caprona frightened
by the closeness of their enemies.
                    I persisted
in meeting the devils' maleficent gaze as I drew
near my guide. They let their hooks drop down
and yelled to one another:

> "How about I hit him in the ass?"

And another said:

> "Sure. Let him have it."

But Viletail still talking to my guide turned
swiftly and said:

> "Down, down, Mussrumple."

Then Mussrumple told us:

"You can't go any further by way of this ridge
because arch six, down below, is shattered. If
you *still* want to go on, make your way
on that cliff; another ridge near here opens
onto a path. Counting back from yesterday—five
hours later than it is now—twelve hundred
sixty-six years had passed since the road buckled.
I'm sending some of my scouts over there
to check and see if anyone's popping out
of the pitch into the drying air. Go with them;
they won't hurt you.
                     Step up here, Bumblebluffer
and Squatterbrine, and you, Mongrelliflare;
Barbaribristle will lead the squad.
                              Now the rest:
Typhoococco, Sneerdragon, you with the tusks—
Hoghunker—and Withersgratte and Lurkowisp
and nutty Ireflush. Check over the boiling pitch
so the travelers can be safe as far as the next ridge
that winds its way whole over the lairs."

I said:

"Oh master, what's this I see? Let's go alone,
please, if you know how. I'd rather do
without escort. If you're as wide-awake
as usual, you can't miss those threatening
brows, the gnashing of those demon-teeth."

And he to me:

"I won't have you be scared; let them gnash away:
it's for the sinners in the stew."

They wheeled about by the bank at the left
but first each one with tongue and
tooth sent a sign to Barbaribristle,
who trumpeted a fart.

TRANSLATOR'S PROCESS NOTES

[All line numbers refer to the Italian text of the Società Danatesca Italiana as published in John Sinclair's edition of the *Inferno;* [] indicate original Italian test; *italics* indicate translations into American. Schwerner's notes indicate that he consulted the *American Heritage Dictionary*, De Luxe Edition for Macintosh, to check or confirm etymologies and definitions. Points where he did so are marked (AHED). Points where he checked his work against the translation of Charles S. Singleton (Dante Alighieri, *The Divine Comedy: Inferno* [Princeton UP, 1970]) are marked "Singleton." Reference to the Reverend Cary is to the translation of *The Divine Comedy* (the first translation of Dante's work into English) by the Reverend Henry Cary, published in 1805. In an interview in *Talisman: A Journal of Contemporary Poetry and Poetics* #19 (1998), Schwerner said that Cary's translation was "in some ways my favorite for a long time, in spite of its expectable early nineteenth century turns, a slighting of the colloquial, inversions of a habitual not a stylistically necessary order. But the translator chose blank verse rather than go towards a doomed effort to ape a *terza rima*. . . .]

CANTO VIII

17. originally I had "I saw approach us,"etc. [venir per l'acqua verso noi]; but remembered a nautical term—: "heave to," particularly apt given the context established by "bowcord, bantam boat, steersman" (heave to, as a nautical term, AHED). I came to think though that this expression was not quite adequate, the more precise idiom being, *heave into sight* or *heave into view* (AHED). This idiom foregrounds the craft as it suddenly comes into the narrator's visual field.

18: [anima fella] literally *wicked, foul, impious* etc. *Wicked soul, foul soul* etc. evokes the rhetoric of 19th c. melodrama. But *gall* seemed interesting (AHED "abnormal swelling of plant tissue," etc., also derivation from Middle English). —thus: *galled soul*. Producing the two English monosyllables' successive vowel sounds requires unusual muscular alignments and buccal shapes, relevant in their relative distortion to the reader's sense of the oarsman's character and cry, a sense intensified by the hieratic contempt implicit in Virgil's utterance—*galled soul*—which takes the measure of the oarsman's demotic *now you've had it.* . . .

19: [tu gridi a voto] literally *you shout emptily:* Singleton: *emptily.* "voto"="vuoto"; but *hollow, empty, void* suggests *shouting into the void*

21: [loto], *slough, muddy sluice, marsh, bog, morass.* But see following note.

21: [passando]: pres. part., fm. passare, *pass by, cross,* etc. I thought of "negotiate" (AHED). The commercial and formal overtones of the Latin-derived *negotiate* seem expresssive of the nature of the brief crossing situation, and contrasts with *fen*'s blunt archaism. (AHED)

22: [Qual è colui che grande inganno ascolta] *taken by* rather than *taken in by: taken* suggests both thralldom and collusion, the latter as *to be taken with*, even though the victim be unaware of the greed generating his own complicity.

23: [e poi se ne rammarca], etc. *in building vexation*, combines the relevant ambiguity of vexation accreting with the suggestion that Phlegyas represents the kind of person who to some degree wilfully irrigates what may appear to others as spontaneously occurring emotionality.

24: [accolta]: *suppressed,* but too abstract and Latinate for the context. So: *damped-down:* (AHED). But then I considered *tamp tr.v., tamped* (AHED).

28: [tosto che 'l duca e io nel legno fui] *embarked* (AHED) seems too formal for the act of stepping into a small boat; definition #2, with *set out,* seems preferable, but doesn't quite give the sense of going into the boat; thus the adoption of the verb *venture* (AHED) with the adverb *down* to accent the deeper riding of the craft, and with the added overtone of Dante and Virgil's overall downward passage.

29-30: continuing the carry of the image: [se ne va l'antica prora dell'acqua piu che . . .] the stress pattern ´ ˘ ´ —amphimacer—was what came to my ear in order to capture the up & down movement of the little boat; in addition I wanted some short, lip-stretching ĭ sounds; thus: *did it dip.* Favoring the more colloquial *went in,* I'd first had *only when I went in did it dip*, but *went in,* ending as it does on a stress, insists on ˘ ˘ ´ as a reading for *did it dip* and works against the pattern ´ ˘ ´. Another sonic mimesis of the boat's vertical movement—doun/wôrn /prou//sô—occurs in the line: *down, the worn prow, sawing ahead, rode* . . . ; the fifth, differento [*rode*] is produced with a near approach to a full round stretching of the lips, the sound suggestive of an exhalation of surprise or admiration, an echo too of the vocative case—followed in turn by the contrasting long, high, pinched *ee* of *deeper*.

31: [morta gora] Singleton: stagnant channel; but I wanted, as I experienced the context, to animize the channel, that is to endow it with its suggestion of a biomorphic high-viscosity horror, à la sci-fi, with harmonics of *clotted* milk, say, or *clotted* artery, *clotted* traffic etc . . . (clot, AHED). Stagnant water's often lumpish.

32: [dinanzi mi si fece un pien di fango] Si fece: preterit, not imperfect; fm. fare, to make, create, produce, thus conceivably *rose, rose up in front of me*, with no necessary imputation of a rising action concurrent with continuous time; thus *manifested,* as of a spirit, v.i.; [pien di fango] full of mud: *crammed, stuffed, arrayed, clothed, enveloped* do not quite suggest the wrinkly invasion of mud around the figure, a muddy "covering" invested as it were, in this Hell, with its own active principle—reminiscent perhaps of the invasiveness of *clot,* above—and thus, *enfolded* is appropriate (AHED) which also—given the overtone of tenderness in the participle—emphasizes through contrast the baseness implicit in the figure's self-presentation and also conveys some of mud's corrugations.

39: [ancor sie lordo tutto] literally *despite all your filth*, but see entry for line 32, above, which suggests a metaphorical continuity in *shrouding muck,* informed too with the monosyllabic powers of the Middle & Old English *muck* (AHED) & *shroud* (AHED).

40: [Allora stese al legno ambo le mani]: [stese] fm. [stendere]: to stretch, to extend, as one's hands, say; but better is the idiom *to reach for,* more adequately conveying his intentions, to reach as if for someone's throat.

41: ['l maestro accorto] literally *wise/shrewd/sagacious/wary master;* most á propos would seem the action-stance stemming from Virgil's attentiveness; thus *alert,* particularly since most of the other adjectival choices suggest a shrewd rather than an aware

Virgil, an attribution not congruent with Dante's esteem for and presentation of his guide.

42: [via costà con li altri cani!] literally *away there with the other dogs!* Idiomatically preferable is *Get back, with all the other dogs.*

44: [alma sdegnosa] literally *indignant soul;* our current, somewhat pejorative sense of *indignant,* which comes perhaps from this century's pervasive and reductive psychologism—"What's he <u>really</u> feeling? What's the <u>real</u> reason for his indignation?"—can't convey Virgil's admiration for Dante's seemingly cruel utterance; in addition, *indignant soul* conveys to modern ears nothing so much as the language of melodrama; *How seemly, soul, your indignation* . . . (seemly, AHED). Note also the syntactical parallel between the narrator's *You, damned* . . . and Virgil's next utterance, *how seemly, soul.* . . .

65-66: [ma nell' orrechie mi percosse un duolo,
      per ch' io avante l'occhio intento sbarro.]
[mi percosse un duolo] [percosse] *broke, crashed, percussed; drove into my ears* seemed barely possible; then I conceived of sounds as waves, thus the wailing waves of sound entering Dante's ears, but the image needed a verb more potently incarnating [mi percosse] in sound and meaning; thus *waves breaking upon a shore, a beach, ramparts;* and, finally, *broke violently / upon my ears*. But what was it that broke? *grief wailing, mourning, cries* . . . ? Working inside the possibilities of Anglo-Saxon or Old Irish etymologies with their associated epic harmonics, I remembered my use of *keening* at the beginning of Canto V; thus: *But a keening broke violently* . . .

[sbarro l'occhio . . .] literally, as Singleton points out, and as the Reverend Cary wrote in the first, 1805, translation into English, *unbar my eye*. The idea of "barring" suggests undoing an obstacle to clear seeing, leading to *washing* or *clearing* or, then, *dropping the scales from one's eyes;* that cliché abandoned, then I considered some kind of removal of the impediment to perception, *wiping, cleaning*—thus: *wiping clear,* less cumbersome than the otherwise suggestive, and literal, [unbar] . . . *a keening broke violently / upon my ears* . . . *I peer ahead*: (percosse . . . sbarro): Dante joins the past absolute with the present, not only in this sequence.

69: [gravi cittadin] Singleton: "gravi cittadin: sinners of lower Hell." English *grave* carries little of the probable imputation; ?dark dwellers ?dark denizens ?dark inhabitants ?heavy town-dwellers: their essential state is total dependence, so unless [cittadin] is ironic—which it may well be—the noun *subjects* might suit better, teamed with the adjective *lowering* (AHED). So we retain some sense of [gravi] serious or grave, but *lowering* offers appropriate contextual harmonics and features a mournful music, as well as the reminder of the shades' Hell-site. However, after all this, it seemed to me that in effect Virgil's comment is ironic! thus: *sober subjects, grand battalions.*

73-74: ['l foco eterno/ch'entro l'affoca le dimostra rosse] Keeping to Dante's <u>endless, makes them show red, to make red-hot,</u> and making clear that the fire was not inside the mosques but within the walls of Dis. *They redden, set aglow by the city's endless fire* or

They're set in a red glow by the city's endless fire
The reddening glow suffuses them   or

The suffusing red they show
The reddening glow suffuses them   or

Reddening and scorched by the city's endless fire,
you can see they're suffused in a glow in this lower Hell   or

Glowing by the city's endless fire, they're suffused
in a red, as you see, in this lower Hell   or

Set aglow by the city's endless fire, they're
suffused with redness, as you see, in this lower Hell

and finally:

"Made other by the city's endless fire,
they're aglow, as you see, with a suffusing
redness in this lower Hell."

100: [disfatto] literally *undone;* the French "délabré" came to me, its meaning essentially "tattered," which on checking I found had as its primary meaning "tattered, as with clothing etc."; thus I considered *don't leave me so tattered* but continued; as a secondary listing the dictionary offers *disorder*; and then I thought of *Lear*, the comment by Regan or Goneril deriding the King's men-at-arms, men so "disordered, so debauch'd and bold" and I stayed with:

> don't leave me so disordered.

CANTO IX

11.1-3: *craven, my face wan, my guide turned away   pushed pressed prodded*

As to Virgil's suppressed "vexation, anger," [il suo novo] "his own new color" (Singleton), see below.

Craven, my face wan
turned away
craven, my face wan, my guide turned away   pushed pressed prodded

My face was wan, prompted by my cravenness:
I was watching my spurned guide
in his turning; swiftly he snuffed/? quelled
his own new tint of quickening vexation.

My guide was turning; seeing my wan face
prompted by cravenness—my spurned guide
swiftly checked the rising tint of his quickened
vexation.

Finally these drafts gave rise to:

> *My guide was turning; seeing my craven face*
> *grow wan as I saw him spurned, he swiftly*

checked the tinted rise of his quickened
vexation.

Note the power inherent in the archaic resonances of *turn, craven, grow, wan, spurn, check, tint, rise, quicken,* characterized by Old or Middle English origins; in addition, the presence of major words stemming from Latin or Greek , *e.g. vexation* (vex, AHED, derivation from Middle English, Old French, Latin), can on occasion intimate significant contrasts, as for example in

. . . . *quickened*
vexation:

in which, too, the enjambment serves aspects of the sense, perhaps all the more keenly, given definition #2 of *quickened,* below. The etymological texture thickens with the inclusion of words—*vexation* again—stemming from both Middle English and Greek or Latin or Old French. *turn, craven, grow, wan, spurn, check, tint, rise, quick en,* and *cwicu* (all AHED for derivations).

Dante embeds color as the main subject: [color] subject [pinse] verb; that is [spinse], from [spingere], prod, push, bring out etc.; also [duca] subject [ristrinse] verb *(suppress).* Did I lose something with the transformations guide was turning . . . he checked? Keeping the present participle [veggendo] might lead in English to awkward syntax; in addition I wanted to juxtapose a past continuous *was turning* with the simple past tense of the powerfully freighted Middle English/Arabic/Persian monosyllable *check.* I emphasized a near-simultaneity with *as I saw him spurned,* the participle rhyming internally with *was turning,* the verb embodying Virgil's unhappy movement. . . . *tinted rise*: conveys Dante's [il suo novo] "his own new color" {Singleton}, along with the overtone of a reaction that is angry or irritated (AHED). Cf. Singleton's Notes: "a flush of vexation and anger, . . ." Here I thought was a legitimate and useful interpretive addition: *vexation.* . . .

1.8: [cominciar] beginning. *start* yields both *beginning* and, most appositely, "a startled reaction or movement"(AHED, derivation from Middle English, Old English).

1.51: [i' mi strinsi al poeta] *I drew near, I presssed close to, I held the poet close.* Best probably *I clutched at* (AHED).

67

CANTO X

11.64-66:

*I knew his name already from what I could intuit
from his words and what I could read in the elements
of his painful sanctions.*

                            (painful, AHED)

*From what I could construe from his words
and what I could read in the elements of his
painful sanctions*

*Because I knew his name I could answer
unstintingly, having already construed
his words and the make-up of his painful
sanctions.*

                           (make-up, AHED)

and finally:

*Having already construed his words
and the make-up of his painful sanctions,
I knew his name and I could answer
unstintingly.*

11.73-75:

        *But that other, great-hearted,
whose 'linger in this place, please,' was staying
me, appeared unchanged, head steady, body fixed*

    expression unvarying   unaltering constant, consistent, unfailing, invariable
unvaried in his look was stolid in expression, unbending in

68

But that great-hearted other's 'linger in this place, please,'
had stayed me, his face now stolid, head unmoving,
body set

But I'd been stayed by that great-hearted other's
'linger in this place, please,' his face now stolid,
head unmoving, body set.

finally:

But I'd been stayed by
great-hearted Farinata's 'linger in this place,
please.' His face now stolid, head unmoving,
body set, he took up where he'd left off

11.77-78: [S'elli han quell'arte male appresa,
        ciò mi tormenta più che questo letto]

I first thought to work with the verbs *suffer* and *pain*, as in examples 1 and 2:

1. "*I suffer more from their deficient study*
of the returner's art than I do from this bed;"

2. "*Their deficient study of the returner's art*
pains me more than this bed;"

Upon further reflection, I found no adequate reason to change the introductory if-clause [s'elli . . .], which may be read as trembling on the edge of not quite admitting the supposition, as if to say "Well, if they <u>really</u> couldn't get it together . . .":

If they've been poor students of die returner's art,
this bed hurts me less than they do

                                  but better the verb *study* than the verb *have been*
—so I came to:

> *If they've studied the returner's art poorly,*
> <u>*that*</u> *torments me more than this bed*

also here the masculine ending *bed*, following the weak syllable *-ly*, fits stress to content.

1.81: [pesa] fm. [pesare], to weigh. But here, as noun: *charge* (AHED, derivation from Middle English, Old French, Latin, Celtic).

CANTO XXI

ll. 4-5: [. . . per veder l'altra fessura/di Malebolge e li altri pianti vani] literally *to see the vain* or *useless or fruitless lamentations/plaints/tears/cries/wails.* . . . Both [fessura] and [pianti] depend upon [vedere]; I felt the awkwardness in American at *seeing* lamentations, especially when coupled with the concretion of *seeing* the pit. Therefore, I settled on *contemplate*, embodying both sight and speculation (AHED).

1. 5: [pianti vani] *vain,* mostly in the sense of useless, as *a vain effort,* probably with some additional overtone suggesting *contemptible*—but yet another overtone of *vain,* namely when a person is overly proud of his accomplishments or his appearance, botches the double thrust suggested above. Thus: *worthless* (AHED).

LL.7-18: cf. the Italian text:

> [Quale nell' arzanà de' Viniziani
>   bolle l'inverno la tenace pece
>   a rimpalmare i legni lor non sani,
> —che navicar non ponno, e in quella vece
>   chi fa suo legno novo e chi ristoppa
>   le coste a quel che più vïaggi fece;
> chi ribatte da proda e chi da poppa;
>   altri fa remi e altri volge sarte;
>   chi terzeruolo e artimon rintoppa—
> tal, non per foco, ma per divin' arte,

70

<blockquote>
bollìa là giuso una pegola spessa,
che 'nviscava la ripa d'ogni parte]
</blockquote>

To adequately render this complex metaphor—which features a parenthetical, itemized sequence—in appropriate American syntax, I substituted the following elements, subject in every case to the Italian context and duplicating or clearly echoing the original meanings; these elements supplied are shown by an underline:

As <u>artisans</u> at the Venice Arsenal boil
gluey pitch in wintertime to stop up
their <u>run-down dry-docked</u> ships—
one <u>worker</u> building his craft anew,
another caulking his <u>travel-weary</u> vessel's
ribs, this <u>artisan</u> hammering away
at the prow, that one at the stern,
others making oars, some twining strands
of hemp, a <u>worker</u> patching a jib
and a mainsail—
                so not by dint of fire . . . etc.

In addition the hyphenated adjectives <u>run-down</u> and <u>dry-docked</u>, two spondees, serve appropriately to slow down the pace of the poem, as does *stop up*.

For the following demon-names, I list—in italics—some preliminary tentative translations.

11. 105-118 and fol.:

MALEBRANCHE: *Vileclaw*

MALACODA: *Viletail*

SCARMIGLIONE: (neologism, from Scarmigliare: dishevel, rumple or muss one's hair) ***Mussrumple***

ALICHINO: from hellequin/arlecchino "harlequin," a ludicrous or bumbling person; a fool. (buffoon, AHED, Old Italian deriavtion) *Pufferwag* **Bumblebuffer**

CALCABRINA: brine-treader. [calca]:craven/crowd/throng/tread/press [brina]/hoarfrost/hoary. *Saltsquatter Trodsalter* **Squatterbrine**

BARBARRICIA: bearded etc. *Bristlechum;* **Barbanbristle**

LIBICOCCO: [libeccio]: south-west wind, and [sirocco]: (sirocco, AHED) zephyr tornado storm sirocco hurricane wind dust dry tsunami typhoon cyclone. *tsunasprinkle Hurricalone Tornarocco* **Typhoococco**

DRAGHIGNAZZO: dragon + *sghignazzare*—to sneer. **Sneerdragon**

CIRIATTO: [ciro] hog. [atto]: act/deed/attitude. **Hoghunker**

GRAFFIACANE: Scratch/scratcher + dog/hound (withers, AHED, derivativation from Middle English, Old English). *gratte-ciel* Fr. sky-scraper **Withersgratte**

CAGNAZZO: [cagna] : dog/bitch. [cagnesco]: hostilely dog-cur-bitch-hostility. *mongrorwath mongrorage raverkanis canoraver* **Mongrelliflare**

FARFARELLO: [folletto]: malevolent spirit or phantom. Cf. Singleton XXX, 32 ghost/goblin (wisp, AHED) *SmutWisp PusWisp Lurk-o'-the-Wisp* **Lurkowisp**

RUBICANTE: rubiginous (AHED, derivation from Latin). **Ireflusher**

Thus:
Vileclaw
Mussrumple
Viletail
Bumblebuffer
Mon grelliflare

Withersgratte
Squatterbrine
Sneerdragon
Hoghunker
Lurkowisp
Barbaribristle
Ireflush
Typhoococc

Designed by
Samuel Retsov

Text: 11pt Perpetua
Titles: 18 pt Imperium

acid-free paper

Printed by
McNaughton & Gunn